LEGENDS OF WARFARE

AVIATION

Short Stirling

RAF Heavy Bomber in World War II

RON MACKAY

SCHIFFER MILITARY

4880 Lower Valley Road   Atglen, PA 19310

Designed by Justin Watkinson
Type set in Impact/Minion Pro/Univers LT Std

ISBN: 978-0-7643-6463-1
Printed in China

Published by Schiffer Publishing, Ltd.
4880 Lower Valley Road
Atglen, PA 19310
Phone: (610) 593-1777; Fax: (610) 593-2002
Email: Info@schifferbooks.com
www.schifferbooks.com

For our complete selection of fine books on this and related subjects, please visit our website at www.schifferbooks.com. You may also write for a free catalog.

Schiffer Publishing's titles are available at special discounts for bulk purchases for sales promotions or premiums. Special editions, including personalized covers, corporate imprints, and excerpts, can be created in large quantities for special needs. For more information, contact the publisher.

We are always looking for people to write books on new and related subjects. If you have an idea for a book, please contact us at proposals@schifferbooks.com.

Contents

Introduction

The necessary advance from single- to multiengine aircraft with which to launch and sustain a bombing campaign against the industrial resources of an adversary began to take comprehensive shape among the major future belligerents across the globe as the 1930s evolved. Several, including Germany, and its Axis partners Italy and Japan, would not largely advance beyond twin-engine designs. In the former nation's case, the perceived priority was to beat its enemies on the battlefield, in which case there would be no need for strikes at an opponent's industrial base when given its inability to sustain the conflict following a military capitulation. The relatively short-to-medium-range nature of such activities meant that there was no need to produce bombers beyond this degree of engine provision, since the crews would not basically be engaged in large-scale, long-range sorties. The Italians and Japanese tended to follow in their partners' footsteps.

Although Britain and American did to a degree follow an initial similar path, in both instances there were influential military and government bodies that looked beyond the tactical aspect of airpower and pressured for a parallel strategic plan that merited the introduction of four-engine bombers. Military history now confirms the basic wisdom of taking up such a stance, as the ultimate ruination of Hitler's Third Reich structure has revealed— an action that arguably could not have succeeded without the existence of the RAF's Lancaster and Halifax fleet along with their US Army Air Force B-17 and B-24 contemporaries.

A third four-engine RAF design entering the lists of strategic combat has still not enjoyed the same public exposure as the Avro and Handley-Page duo, this being the Short Stirling. Its initial paper existence under Air Ministry specification B12/36, relating to a four-engine design, ironically placed it ahead of the two abovementioned bombers at this stage. The Halifax's P13/36 specification related to a twin-engine aircraft, while the Lancaster emerged from the twin-engine Manchester, ordered under the same specification as the Halifax. That the Lancaster and Halifax evolved as four-engine contemporaries of the Stirling was down to respective operational and technical factors. The failure of the Manchester in service and a shortage of the Rolls-Royce Vulture (ironically, the same power source for the Avro twin that played a prominent part in its failure), resulting in the Halifax switching to four Rolls-Royce Merlin engines, were the thankfully positive results.

B13/36 introduced a second form of takeoff ability; namely, the use of catapult equipment assistance to supplement normal procedure; the suggested reasoning was that greater fuel loads and bombloads could be accommodated in the latter case. Normal takeoff requirements were 1,500 miles with a 2,000-pound bombload; catapult assistance increased the foregoing figures to 2,000 or 3,000 miles with respective bombloads of 14,000 and 8,000 pounds. The all-up-weight (AUW) factors were 31,200 or 36,000 pounds. A further refinement was the need to clear a 50-foot height within a mere 1,500-foot takeoff run, which left a key need for maximum engine output and wing area.

Catapult assistance was deemed necessary in these perceived circumstances, given the then-current grass-surfaced and relatively limited dimensions of most RAF airfields prior to World War II. In the event, the Stirling would function in normal takeoff circumstances while accommodating a greatly enhanced AUW reaching 70,000 pounds that also accommodated bombloads up to 14,000 pounds (of course, the existence of concrete runways within noticeably larger dimensioned airfields over the ensuing five years presented a lesser albeit not totally absent challenge to the average bomber's takeoff performance by the early 1941 operational debut of the Stirling).

The S31/M4 was the designation for what was a half-scale version of the future Short Stirling, which was utilized to evaluate the aerodynamic characteristics of the aircraft. The aircraft's dimensions allowed for the application of a standard landing-gear frame. Prewar airfields' restricted layouts coupled with an inability to alter the wing angle with which to accommodate the single-stage landing gear seen here forced the adaptation of a double-stage frame on the second full-size prototype.

A grainy-quality photograph of the half-scale Stirling design is seen as it is completing the landing approach. The background detail, allied to the grass surface of the airfield, presents the impression of a countryside landscape rather than an aviation-oriented scene. The S31/M4 was unfortunately written off following a heavy landing during World War II.

A marginally more angular view of the half-scale aerofoil shows off the wing pattern adapted from the Sunderland flying boat. The airframe, unlike its metal-clad full-size successor, was wood based in nature. The aircraft was consequently a pleasure to fly, given the enhanced power-to-weight ratio. Note the designator detail on the fin and rudder.

The full-scale Stirling prototype L7600 provides a better indication of the steeper ground angle compared to the original fitting seen on the S1/M4 airframe. National markings are confined to fuselage and upper wing roundels. The aircraft inaugural flight occurred on May 13, 1939, the date proving to live up to its jinx reputation.

Landing-gear failure traced to the light-alloy back arch braces (replaced by tubular steel units on subsequent aircraft) was the cause of L7600's premature demise. Structural damage adding to the dislodgement of the no. 2 engine was of a scale to render the airframe as category E, fit only for salvage.

A forward-angle depiction of the fourth production Mk. I N3638 provides a better impression of the sheer size of the bomber, with the cockpit height around 22 feet above the airfield surface. The dark-green/dark-earth upper camouflage contrasts with the yellow-sprayed undersides denoting a trials status. Aircraft has nose and tail gun turrets but lacks the projected ventral fitting. Bell-pattern spinners on early-series Mk. Is. were discontinued from late Mk. I Series I airframes onward. Engine exhaust pipes on outer cowling surfaces were soon standardized to a common starboard location.

The company's response envisioned a midwing airframe of metal stressed skin powered by Rolls-Royce Goshawk steam-cooled engines, which would give way to the Bristol Hercules air-cooled radial format. Crew complement was set at two pilots, an observer/navigator, a wireless operator, and two gunners. Subsequent complements rose to eight with the splitting of the observer/navigator roles and the World War II introduction of a flight engineer; finally, the latter specialist's introduction led to the deletion of the second-pilot function, with the engineer assisting the pilots on takeoff and landing to create a seven-man team that saw out the conflict.

Defensive armament comprised two power turrets, a nose-mounted FN5 with two machine guns, and a quadruple-gun arrangement in an FN4A, which later changed to an FN20A equivalent unit. A third defensive measure anticipated the aircraft countering attacks from a ventral direction; a remote-control turret under the rear fuselage was the planned antidote, but this feature never extended beyond a single manual unit in the Mk. I Series I production run. (To a diminution in speed when the FN25A was in the lowered position was added an even more inhibiting ground action; the leaking of the hydraulic valves led to the turret sagging, with the gun barrels then prone to impacting with the ground.) The Mk. I Series II airframes were intended to be equipped with two FN55A beam gun mountings that reportedly never were equipped with weapons. Finally, an FN7A middle upper turret appeared on the

Mk. I, Series III airframes, and the three-turret arrangement became standard on all subsequent Mk. I and III airframes as well as the handful of Mk. IIs. (The circular cover for the original FN25A was retained, in which a single machine gun could be borne, if necessary, but the arrangement appears not to have been a regular application, especially since there was no question of its constant manning unless an extra gunner was carried.)

A forward view of the cockpit area with the pilots' seats still to be installed allows a focus on the two marginally tapered control columns with circular handgrips; the pedestal frame in the center is the base for the banks of levers with which to operate the engine throttles, flaps, landing gear, etc. Access to the nose compartment is just visible at the base of the photograph.

The pilots' seats are now fitted, with both showing the shoulder straps for when they are flying the aircraft. Left-hand first pilot's seat has a hinged armored frame in the folded-down position, a luxury not accorded his colleague. The cockpit base frame was raised above the main fuselage floor, with access to the nose compartment in the center. The forward edge of the navigator's table is just visible at lower left.

CHAPTER 1
Mk. I Prototype: Development, Construction, and Production

Although preceding its contemporaries in four-engine terms and possessing equal theoretical range and load capacity, it was to be the Stirling's fate not to see out World War II in the same primary bomber role. There would be two major technical or design limitations that would ensure this negative aspect of operational function:

1. The projected fuselage dimensions of the Stirling were prodigious by any World War II standard, let alone those envisaged in 1936. A fuselage length of 87 feet, 3 inches, within which was enclosed a bomb bay around half of this figure (42 feet), was to prove well ahead of the Halifax and even the Lancaster in equivalent statistics. The overall structure was completed in four sections, three being 25 feet, to permit loading on RAF transport vehicles such as the *Queen Mary*. They were of semirectangular cross section, with lower section spars inserted level with the internal decking. This base was in turn supported by two longitudinal beams. The downside to the latter facility, compared to the respective 33-foot and 22-foot single-cell layout on the Lancaster and Halifax, was the presence of the beams intruding down from the bomb bay roof. The current range of bombs went up only to the 500-pounder, although there was a 2,000-pound, slim-line, armor-piercing weapon. The trio of lateral space limitations posed by the beams' presence did not inhibit any of these missiles from being hoisted into position. However, as World War II's progress resulted in ever-larger and greater-girth bombs being introduced, this layout simply prevented their carriage. Conversely, the striking power of the bulk of prewar explosive weaponry proved incapable of creating severe damage to industrial, transportation, or military structures of other than marginal scale, a factor that further diminished the Stirling in adding to the offensive. The one portable weapon that could provide a supporting measure of destruction was the incendiary bomb.

2. The need for an equally large wing structure to support the planned fuselage was pitched by the Short management at 110 feet in span, but what was to prove another operational inhibition related not to the bomber's flight time but to whenever hangar stowage for more-detailed maintenance was deemed necessary. The Air Ministry's counterproposal required a span under 100 feet, this being based on the fact that the maximum width of RAF hangars stood at this stated size. However, the planned width expansion to 120 feet for the type C and D hangars, which were to prove the centerpieces of RAF permanent airfields, would clearly accommodate the required wingspan, and these structures would be in regular numbers by the start of World War II. No apparent consideration was given to this advance, and the result was a structure clearly based on the wing pattern fitted to the Short Sunderland flying boat. The consequence was an increase in wing load per square foot that was to critically penalize performance in terms of maximum altitude as well as climb rate.

The long-range nature of Sunderland operations ensured the fuel capacity was accordingly high. A total of 2,254 gallons were shared between fourteen wing tanks, whose disposition was four and three, respectively, serving the inner and outer engines on either wing. They were positioned in groups of four directly behind the engines, two toward the wings' rear section and with the seventh within the wing leading edge between the fuselage and inner engine; all but the seventh were self-sealing, but this exception was rarely used unless completing a maximum-range sortie. The six bomb cells, spread between the fuselage and inner engine nacelles, could hold ferry tanks, the extra capacity therein amounting to 219 gallons. A potentially positive structural inclusion was the introduction of watertight outer wing sections that would assist the aircraft in remaining afloat in the event of a ditching. Balloon-cable cutters were installed in the wing leading edges.

Mini Stirling

Unlike standard prototype procedure, the Short hierarchy built a half-scale twin, the S31/M4; it was initially powered by four Pobjoy Niagara III motors, which were subsequently displaced by the Niagara IV, with an extra 15 hp output over its predecessor's 90 hp figure. First flown on September 19, 1938, by the chief test pilot John Lankester Parker, it bore the intended fuselage layout but employed a wing based on the Scion Senior, a similar smaller-scale test bed for the company's civil Empire Flying Boat. Over the following months, all progressed well with the Stirling Minor, other than replacement of the horn-balanced elevators with a normal equivalent that cured the incipient center-of-gravity (C of G) problem.

Early in the test sequence there arose a further issue that would unconsciously create yet another problem, this time centered on the landing gear. The A and AEE staff regarded the S31/M4's takeoff runs as excessive and, foreseeing this basic problem worsening as the Stirling's AUW steadily climbed, requested that the company alter the wing's angle of incidence from what was then 3½ degrees to almost double at 6 degrees. Unfortunately, by the time the request was submitted, the two full-scale prototypes, L7600 and L7605, were deemed to be so far advanced in construction that the desired switch would result in an inordinate time extension coupled with an equally inordinate cost increase.

The single and unwelcome option was to increase the landing-gear length, but in a starkly different manner. The engine nacelle was too limited in length to accommodate a lengthened, single-hinged wheel-support frame. Instead, a second hinge point roughly halfway along the struts' length was fitted. Now, the retraction procedure was for the lower portion to retract back; when in a horizontal position, the entire structure was raised vertically into the nacelle.

The retraction motors originally positioned within the nacelle were subsequently moved into the fuselage; the alteration allowed for manual retraction in the event of mechanical failure. If failure occurred, the crew member concerned only had to crank the gear up, using a handle—with no fewer than 740 turns required! The requisite angle of incidence was accommodated on the S31/M4, but the lengthened landing gear appeared only on the second prototype, L7605. The change was introduced on all production airframes thereafter, albeit at the expense of a potentially frail landing-gear frame that was destined to cast up regular cases of failure, whenever a heavy or wayward landing arose.

Prototype Testing

The foregoing situation was unknown to anybody on May 14, 1939, when the chief test pilot pushed the throttles forward and launched L7600 into the air. All progressed well up aloft, but disaster struck as the prototype touched down. The landing-gear failure that ensued saw the aircraft flop onto its belly, with the no. 2 engine dislodged in the impact; a category E reduction was the result—not the best outcome for the company or the Air Ministry, whose previous decision had been to place an order for one hundred aircraft! As matters transpired, the flight performance of L7605, the second prototype, the following December 3, involving inclusion of the extended landing gear (an item absent

on L7600), passed off in sound order. It was subsequently dispatched to Boscombe Down for evaluation. The concept of catapult launch was by now placed in permanent abeyance.

During the testing sequence, there arose a problem with slow throttle response that contributed to the pilot having to make a three-engine landing. The Exacter throttles, a carryover from the company's flying boats, displayed a clear tendency to shift to a closed position when hand pressure was released. The solution was to apply serrated arcs on the throttle box, and spring-loaded detents on the levers, the combination resulting in the throttles remaining in the required position. Later, the throttles were modified with a hinged top on the levers that when pulled or pushed lifted a spring-loaded detent; this in turn engaged an adjustable stop that set the throttles at cruise power.

Operationally Diminishing Factors

The stage was by now unknowingly being set for the Stirling's overall operational performance to prove seriously wanting in two key scenarios and a third less critical. The wingspan limitation would impose serious restrictions on the bomber's ability to attain an average altitude matching that of its future Avro and Handley-Page contemporaries. The Boscombe Down test sequence at an AUW of 57,400 pounds' ability resulted in a takeoff run of 1,920 feet and a farther 1,680 feet with which to clear a height of 50 feet to attain its operational altitude. Stall speed was 107 indicated airspeed (IAS).

What really proved disappointing was the maximum 15,000 feet in altitude attained—barely half the original requested specification figure. The failure was matched by a climb rate that, although commencing at 300 feet per minute (fpm) up to 5,000 feet, subsequently fell away to a rate that culminated in a meager 160 fpm between 10,000 and 15,000 feet. This overall performance was attributed to the original output of the Hercules II engines at 1,375 hp, but subsequent replacement by the Hercules XI, rated at 1,590 hp, and even by the VI and XVI successors would still leave the Stirling laboring under these restrictions.

The inevitable performance penalties between anticipation and what transpired in practice, which was being posed by ever-increasing AUW totals, witnessed the estimated 327 mph maximum and 282 mph cruising speeds with an 8,000-pound bombload and 59,090 pounds of AUW falling noticeably to 260 mph and 215 mph in operational terms when the Mk. I entered frontline service.

The design of the bomb bay layout was the second limiting factor, in respect of the maximum size of individual bombs capable of being housed therein. Unfortunately, there was no way in which the bay's configuration could be altered, and so the Stirling's ability to deliver a positive explosive weight to the bombing offensive remained permanently degraded. (The sole mass-pattern weapon capable of being borne came from incendiary bomb stocks, with which to reinforce the raids' effect by penetrating the interior of structures previously fractured due to explosive force, so allowing access for further destruction by fire effect.)

The third defect was due to the landing gear's double-hinged layout. Although any landing-gear frame was liable to failure, especially in wayward landing attempts or weather-affected maneuvers, the Stirling's gear layout was especially and inherently susceptible to collapse in other than a normal landing approach.

Monocoque engine nacelle design applied to the first ten Series I production airframes, although aerodynamically beneficial, ironically created problems for maintenance staff, with difficulty regularly arising during engine change. The cure to this was to apply firewalls ahead of the wing leading edges on all other Mk. I production airframes. As for the ten aircraft so equipped, nine were never issued to operational squadrons but served instead as trainers.

Construction

The airframe was all-metal stressed skin in nature, with a fuselage 83 feet, 3 inches length and midset wings spanning 99 feet, 1 inch. The fuselage consisted of four sections, none more than 25 feet in length, measurements reportedly so restricted with which to accommodate loading onto the standard RAF road transport, the *Queen Mary*. The two largest sections were from just ahead of the cockpit windshield to a point several feet ahead of the wing trailing edge; from there, the second equally extended section reached back to just ahead of the stabilizers. The other two reduced-length sections formed the nose and tail. Each section featured continuous-length stringers, and vertical frames at closely spaced intervals were linked up by tension bolts inserted in the end-frame webs. The front main section's spar booms lined up with the interior deck, the latter being borne on longitudinal girders mounted within the 42-foot-long bomb bay to provide three parallel bomb cells that could accommodate 250- or 500-pound standard bombs or the slimline 2,000-pound armor-piercing bomb—a layout destined to impinge upon the design's efficiency when larger World War II weapons proved incapable of stowage due to these space restrictions. An external variation on Mk. I airframes as far along as the first W Series was the absence of the twin pitot masts under the nose compartment.

Interior

The bomb aimer entered the lower nose compartment via the opening positioned between the pilots' seats; the navigator was located directly

A Mk. I Stirling wing is in the process of having the port landing gear attached, with two workers attending to the top vertical aligned section of the overall wheel structure. The bomber's airframe will then be raised up to bring the landing gear into a vertical position. The twin apertures in between the nacelles relate to the original oil cooler intakes, which were transferred to a ventral position on the Hercules XVI nacelles. The space ahead of the N-pattern main-spar frame alongside the inner nacelle accommodates the non-self-sealing 154-gallon fuel tank.

A lateral view of an exposed Stirling inner-wing frame shows up the Warren truss framework between the main spars. The curved strip extending beneath the rear wing frame is the innermost of five roller channels; these match the top curve of the Gouge flaps and link up to roller ribs mounted on the flap surface, with which to control its deployment and retraction.

Stirling production is seen in flow here. What are Mk. I Series I or II airframes, to judge by the absence of "taboo track" frames for middle upper turrets, are progressing steadily toward basic completion. The wing surfaces on the aircraft in the left center reveal the large apertures accessing the fuel tanks, as well as the large-scale Gouge flaps. Fin/rudder and stabilizer frames are still lacking, as are engines and landing gear.

behind the left-hand pilot's seat. Directly behind the armored bulkhead sited below the rear cockpit frame was the wireless operator's position set to port; directly across from him sat the flight engineer, whose equipment was partially positioned ahead of him and partially positioned above the upper section of the front wing-spar support frame. The other major obstruction was the middle upper turret, extending down to near the floor surface, but which could be maneuvered around on either side; an added bonus for the gunner was the ability to gain easy access and, arguably more important, easy exit from his position in an emergency.

The Stirling crews enjoyed little physical advantage in free movement compared to the other two four-engine bombers. Whereas the Halifax's and Lancaster's wing spars were above the bomb bay and therefore provided a barrier to movement along the length of the interior, no such inhibition applied to the Short bomber. However, this advantage was basically nullified by the presence of the wing-spar support frames, whose layout badly limited upright passage down to a crouching posture.

Nevertheless, the relatively open internal layout of the forward and more so the rear fuselage compared to the Halifax, and even more so the Lancaster, provided the best (theoretical) opportunity between the trio of bombers to achieve a swift and, it was hoped, successful evacuation should mortal damage be inflicted by flak or fighters. The forward nose hatch was immediately accessible to the pilot/pilots, bomb aimer, and navigator, as well as the flight engineer and wireless operator; the latter duo could also avail themselves of the roof hatch behind the rear cockpit frame. The rear top hatch ahead of the middle upper turret was equipped with a ladder stowed in the fuselage ceiling, but of necessity was normally used to gain access to the port-wing-positioned dinghy in the event of a ditching. The middle upper gunner could slip out of his turret via the attached ladder much more quickly than his Lancaster contemporary, who was poised several feet up, since he was granted quick exit via the floor escape hatch adjacent to the entrance door.

Only the rear gunner shared a less swift evacuation situation, since all those manning this position on any medium or heavy RAF bomber so outfitted had to go back into the rear fuselage to gain the observer-type parachute packs—the turret's narrow confines preventing attachment while manning their weapons— and clip it to the harness prior to rotating his turret and jumping clear. In practice, the crew-fatality percentage among Stirling crews was to prove little better over the course of the offensive vis-à-vis its contemporaries, and it was rare that more than one or two, let alone the majority of each seven- or eight-man team, reached the ground alive following their aircraft's demise.

The truly gargantuan dimension of the Stirling fuselage in comparison to its future four-engine Bomber Command partners is displayed here. W7508's serial, which will later be displayed in much-smaller format ahead of the stabilizers, is prominently applied around the bomb bay. The aircraft's Mk. I Series III status is confirmed by the presence of the FN7 turret. Picture taken at the Austin Motors plant, with the aircraft the ninth in the second of six batches.

A regular production picture is presented here, with the nearside fuselage confirming its Series III status thanks to the FN7 middle upper turret. Pairs of wings are lined up alongside the fuselages; the first two in the right-side line show off the disposition of the four fuel tank apertures between the engines (*near side*) and on the outer wing area on its companion.

Wings

Unlike the fuselage, which was a distinct switch from flying-boat manufacture, there was little need to construct a new wing structure. Instead, the design team headed by Arthur Gouge in effect borrowed the patterns for the Empire flying boat.

The wing spars formed the front and rear of a tapered box structure extending to where it linked up with the separate wingtip section as the primary core of the overall wing aerofoil. Each of the two inner spar ends linked up to the base and middle of a tubular frame encircling the interior, which additionally possessed a midpositioned horizontal solid strip, from which in turn a V-pattern frame extended down to the fuselage floor to link up with a second horizontal strip.

The trio of wing leading-edge sections was positioned between the fuselage and inner engine nacelle and the inner and outer engine nacelles, as well as between the outer nacelle and the separate wingtip frame (the inner section between the inner engine nacelle and fuselage contained the seventh fuel tank facility).

An overall covering of aluminum alloy sheeting was flush-riveted into place. However, lattice-braced ribs inserted to provide torsion box bracing in the spar truss were an adaptation vis-à-vis the flying-boat equivalent layout. Massive flaps equal to 48 percent of wing chord were proposed by Gouge. These were not hinged

to form the wing undersurface when retracted. Instead, they were complete wing-pattern aerofoils that moved into and out from the main wings on rails.

Twin landing lights that were lowered when in use were positioned in the wing leading edge to the outside of the port outer engine.

Production

The company plant at Rochester in Kent was to be the production source for the Air Ministry's initial order for one hundred airframes, but the "shadow" factory scheme already in force witnessed a second plant at Belfast in Northern Ireland being set up, followed in time by a third at the Austin Motor Co.'s Longbridge location in Birmingham; a further production source at Stoke-on-Trent belonging to the Rootes Co. never materialized. In addition, a number of company concerns adding up to around twenty provided components. The "shadow" concept had anticipated serious disruption by enemy air assault should production be limited to one location, and was a measure destined to be well founded as regular Luftwaffe operations over the UK expanded during 1940–41.

The rate of Stirling turnout was reportedly hindered for some months due to shortages in the requisite machine tools, forgings and extrusions, etc. A further obstruction arose following Britain's military exclusion from the Continent in May–June 1940; Lord Beaverbrook, then in charge of aircraft production, demanded an almost total switch to fighter production in view of the looming threat of invasion should the Luftwaffe gain aerial supremacy over Fighter Command.

Despite this, production did finally commence in mid-1940, but almost immediately the direct threat from aerial action struck home at both company plants. First, on August 14, a nocturnal raid by the specialist KGr. 100 and its He 111s, equipped with X-Gerät, accurately laid their loads upon the Belfast factory, destroying five airframes. Within twenty-four hours, Rochester's production facilities were thoroughly hammered by Do 17Zs of I. and II./KG 3 to leave a further six airframes in ruins. The attacks had delayed the current turnout of Stirlings but were destined never to be repeated, despite Rochester being perilously exposed in terms of accessibility to the bomber airfields in France and Belgium. Germany's industrial structure along with the cities within which production was based had been granted a marginal reprieve from the ever-burgeoning RAF bombing offensive, which would bring massive destruction and human suffering to the unfortunate denizens of Nazi-dominated Germany and her Axis partners.

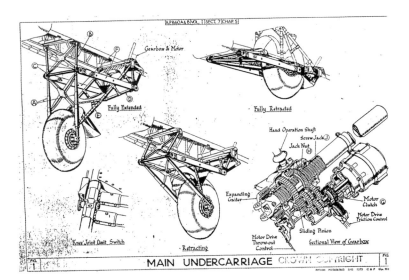

The two-stage landing-gear arrangement peculiar to the Stirling is shown in this diagram. The three stages between full deployment, commencing the retraction action and full stowage within the nacelle, are demonstrated. The retraction gearbox and motor location seen at the top of the left-hand drawing were later transferred into the fuselage to enable manual action of the landing gear's movement should the motor fail.

CHAPTER 2
Mk. I Operations

No. 3 Group, based in East Anglia, was to become the operational source for the Stirling, with newly reformed No. 7 Squadron receiving its first example during August; the squadron was at the time located farther north at Leeming, Yorkshire, and would transfer to Oakington, north of Cambridge, only two months later. Six further squadrons would convert onto the Mk. I during 1941 and 1942. However, the seventh No. 3 Group–assigned unit, No. 620, would do so only between its formation in June 1943 and the following November, when it would transfer out of Bomber Command to No. 38 Group, a transport-functioning entity, although retaining its Stirling establishment of aircraft; the bomber variant on hand by then was the Mk. III.

By February 1941, there were two four-engine bomber squadrons on hand, with No. 35 (Madras) Squadron in No. 4 Group having received its Handley-Page Halifax complement at Linton-on-Ouse, Yorkshire, in late 1940. The race was on for the honor of inaugurating the future four-engine-based offensive, and it would be No. 7 Squadron that was the winner by several weeks (both units would subsequently be their group representatives in the formation of No. 8 [PFF] Group during August 1942).

However, this contest could have been lost due to prolonged problems with the initial cadre of bombers, which were powered by the inadequate output delivered by their Hercules II motors; this primary malady was coupled to Exactor throttle delay in response, burnout of the landing-gear-retraction motor, oil leaks, and other failures. The range of problems ensured that a prolonged period elapsed during which the bombers on squadron hand were declared nonoperational. It was several weeks into 1941 before final clearance was granted for operations to commence.

On February 11, the briefing for a raid on oil storage tanks at Rotterdam was completed, an arguably low-key debut. Forty-three bombers were dispatched as a diversion force for over two hundred striking at Hannover; among the former number were just three Stirlings, whose crews discharged their loads, with no overall losses suffered.

Whether they had participated in this or the Main Force effort, the stark fact was that the likelihood of accurate bombing over Hannover or any other target with no geographic identity was unknowingly almost zero at this time. RAF navigational facilities were incapable of assisting the crews in gaining even approximate let along direct access to the location to be assaulted. It would be a full year or more before the command would see its fortunes even marginally turning in favor of achieving regular target access, after which increasing electronic-equipment availability commencing from early 1943 on would irresistibly turn the screw on the enemy's resources.

No. 7 Squadron's Stirlings were joined on operations by those of No. 15 Squadron during late April, followed by No. 149, whose operational debut was November 26–27. Losses during this operational spell for Bomber Command were casting up a worrying increase, and the Stirling was inevitably bearing a proportion within this figure. The lack of a bomber stream allowed the Nachtjagd crews free scope in conjunction with initial ground and, later, onboard radar to close in on and dispatch their solo-flying and accordingly vulnerable adversaries. Even the three-gun turret Mk. I Series III Stirlings (the FN7 middle upper turret having previously been absent on the Series I and II) were not guaranteed to survive the cannon and bullet fusillade delivered by the Bf 110s on current hand—and that was assuming the gunners were fortunate enough to pick out their assailant in time to raise a challenge of any kind.

The lower nose compartment was home for the bomb aimer, with ample space in which to operate his bombsight, which focused via the center Plexiglas frame. The bomb-bay control box frame is to the right, while the airman's parachute pack is stowed in the shelf (*left*). The FN5 nose turret was also in his charge whenever he was free to do so.

A squad of what is British army as opposed to RAF personnel is swinging right under the starboard wing of a Mk. I Stirling. The aircraft is an initial Series I airframe as confirmed by the spinner covers, which were deleted from subsequent Series I, II, and III airframes. The absence of the ventral-positioned pitot masts does not necessarily indicate a grounded aircraft, since photographs reveal a similar absence on airworthy examples from this production group.

The loading of bombs into an anonymous Stirling's bomb bay clearly illustrates the reason why the bomber could not accommodate weapons of a greater girth than approximately 2 feet. Note also the three wing-mounted cells, which are being simultaneously loaded. Three identification lights are positioned directly behind the front of the bomb bay.

The question of the Short design's inadequate altitude capability was ironically not so critical a feature at this stage of the offensive. Its twin-engine partners usually operated at a similar altitude, which in turn would be noticeably below that of the Lancaster and Halifax. This basic deficiency for the Stirling crews would sadly be only magnified when it, along with its four-engine partners, fully assumed the campaign's function following the withdrawal of the Hampden, the Whitley, and, later, the Wellington from operations. Only then would the altitude factor consistently strike home; the existence of the bomber stream from 1942 onward would literally leave the Stirling out in the cold, with its inability to gain and sustain the altitude capability of its partners, accordingly leaving it exposed to aerial interdiction from flak and even more so from Nachtjagd attention.

A variation, however small scale, from flying nocturnal operations arrived early in the Stirling's career. The creation of "Circus" operations with which to bring the Luftwaffe's Bf 109s and, later, Fw 190s up to challenge Fighter Command was centered on a small force of bombers enmeshed in a virtual web of Spitfires and Hurricanes, with the latter taking on and vanquishing their adversaries. The initial use of Blenheims then gave way to the Stirling, although their numbers were equally small. The restricted range of the fighters ensured that operations were conducted over northeastern France, which resulted in an attendant dearth of suitable targets. The almost inevitable result was for the enemy fighters to indulge in feints and swift forays against the RAF formations; a worse knock-on result was a casualty rate of over two to one in favor of the Jagdwaffe, especially following the introduction of the Fw 190, whose overall performance was a quantum leap ahead of even the Mk. V Spitfire.

Secret Trials over Brest

The sustained assault on the Kriegsmarine warships *Scharnhorst*, *Gneisenau*, and *Prinz Eugen*, bottled up in the French port of Brest during 1941 and early 1942, witnessed the Stirling's participation, albeit with a marginal difference to its bomber contemporaries, whose regular brief was pure bombing. Several of the Stirlings, in contrast, were involved with the operational trial of a device that would evolve into a largely accurate blind marker system over designated targets. The gestation period culminating in the appearance of what was code-named "Oboe" had commenced in late 1941, but the concept on which it was based dated back to the Blitz and the Luftwaffe's use of the X-Gerät blind-bombing system. The German intersecting twin-beam layout provided for a daunting degree of accuracy and was adapted by a TRE (Telecommmunications Research Establishment) team

headed by Dr. Reeves and E. F. Jones; the system consisted of a modified CHL (Chain Home Low) station and a fighter IFF (identification friend or foe) providing the bomb-release point and further employed the Bailie beam, a Farnborough development along which the aircraft tracked to the target. The equipment was set up in Cornwall, with a view toward evaluating its effectiveness against the battleship trio nestling in Brest. The Stirlings so outfitted were part of an overall bomber force, the intention being to conceal the experimental flights from coming to the Germans' attention; all produced very precise results, without any bombers being lost. However, the crews involved came from No. 109 Squadron, which had emerged in 1940 from the Wireless Intelligence Development Unit (WIDU). The latter unit had been created to examine and, if possible, counter the malign effect of the Luftwaffe's trio of blind-bombing devices; their research commenced with Knickebein in mid-1940 and extended to X- and Y-Gerät. Bombing the transmitters and jamming were the twin measures utilized, with the latter proving more effective.

Millennium

Air Chief Marshal Arthur "Butch" Harris's assumption of command in February 1942 witnessed Bomber Command at a nadir in fortunes, with little tangible effect on Nazi Germany's industrial fabric and calls for its unconscious dilution in effort through direct subordination to naval and army requirements. He had already created the bomber stream concept, with which to swamp the Nachtjagd defensive network, but what he then needed was a demonstration of his force's true value, if the siren calls for dispersal were to be permanently silenced. He came up with what was to prove a catalyst in striking power by proposing a raid involving no fewer than a thousand aircraft, Operation Millennium. The risk of mass collisions among the nocturnally launched mass plus an equal risk of sizable losses to the night fighters was balanced by the punishment expected to be administered to the target, in this case the industrial city of Cologne.

A perceived necessity was for the target to be well illuminated either by flares or the quick ignition through incendiary effect by the leading stream elements. The formation of No. 8 (PFF) Group was still several months away, so ignition was the better option. The complete Stirling establishment of Nos. 7, 15, 149, 214, and 218 Squadrons at the time went aloft, although No. 7 was back within the main formation. The lead force crews would share the task of igniting Cologne along with several Wellington squadrons, and it was two No. 15 Squadron Stirlings that first penetrated the Kammhuber Himmelbett screen and closed in on the city center. Their successful discharge could have been compromised by dummy fire sites, but their strike was thankfully and swiftly backed up to provide a literal beacon for the hundreds of the main force crews. The result was a stunningly thorough pounding of the city's hitherto virtually untouched industrial and commercial facilities, at an amazingly low cost of forty-one out of 1,047 bombers dispatched. Although two subsequent 1,000-bomber raids proved very varied in results, the die was now cast not only for Bomber Command's survival but also its future buildup as a viable strike force.

The Pathfinders

The pressing need for a specialist subforce of bombers to precede the main force, with a view to accurately marking targets, finally came to fruition in mid-1942; this was despite Harris's initial opposition on the grounds that the result would be the siphoning off of the best crews in main force squadrons, with a negative effect on the units so affected by such transfers out. The cadre of squadrons chosen to initiate what was later titled No. 8 Pathfinder Force (PFF) Group involved four, each operating on different aircraft designs and at the time based with Nos. 1, 3, 4, and 5 Groups. In No. 3's case it was the Oakington-based No. 7 Squadron that was selected, which would serve in the role up to VE-day. (No. 5 Group's 83 Squadron would be dispatched back from No. 8 Group in 1944 to form the basis for the group's separate PFF force, as would be No. 97 Squadron.)

An initial lack of specialist marker flares coupled to the crews' immediate operational debut, with no time granted for even basic training in the activity, resulted in a number of raids that were failures, although there were several surprising successes between the group's August debut and the year's end. The expanding presence of the Lancaster and Halifax at the time, with their superior altitude capability, was clearly casting up the Stirling's vulnerability to assault in these circumstances, but nothing could be done to ameliorate the bombers' isolation from the stream and attendant heightened risk of dispatch by aerial or flak-based means. (The 1,500 hp, two-stage Hercules XIs mounted on the Series III airframes could bring the Mk. I up to a maximum of 16,000 feet, but even then, this often left the bombers flying within the lower reaches of the stream at best.)

Gardening

A secondary albeit important duty for the RAF bombers was the laying of mines along the western coastline of Europe, as well as into the Baltic. This was conducted with a view to disrupting Germany's shipping traffic, with commercial vessels primarily in mind. Commencing in late 1940, the duty gradually evolved from the trio of first-generation heavies, with the Hampden a particular choice, to the four-engine successors.

This was a function that the Stirling could share in; the relatively narrow diameter of the weapons coupled with the lengthy bomb bay allowed for the carriage of a sizable number of the mines. The activity was given the whimsical title of "Gardening" since the sea formed a marine version of a land-based plot into which they could be planted.

What might appear at first sight to be a less parlous form of operations proved to be far from the case. First, the laying of mines required a low-level approach to the area to be sown, as it were, and required sound navigation to the briefed stretch of sea. The sea routes along which the vessels plied their trade were of necessity not far distant from the coast. The relative lack of airspace in which to maneuver was accordingly restricted for the aircraft should they have the misfortune to intrude upon a convoy while conducting their nocturnal task.

Second and even more crucial were the flak ships, which usually escorted the merchantmen and the foregoing low-altitude limitation on evasive action should battle be joined, which set the survival odds firmly against the RAF airmen; bailing out was virtually impossible to survive at low altitude, and ditching was the sole option—assuming this drastic emergency act could be

What is a Series I Mk. I with propeller spinner covers has several ground crew gathered around as the airman in the cockpit prepares to start up. The individual directly behind the landing gear is sitting on the auxiliary power unit (APU), which is plugged in to initiate start-up and whose use saves the aircraft's internal power system. The extremely low camouflage separation line was later raised toward the top of the fuselage on later production airframes.

A close view of the solid rear frame on an FN7 turret has been shot from the rear of the cockpit. The small rectangular panel can be jettisoned to allow the gunner to bail out, but the meager proportions of the potential exit suggest that the task would prove virtually impossible.

A reverse view of the same bomber picks out the turret front with the machine gun slots. The heavy framing must have provided a dangerously restricted view other than to directly forward. Note the rear rim of the taboo track cover, which elevated the guns when aligning with any point on the airframe.

safely carried out, but it often proved to be fatal. The proximity of the land could see further deadly interdiction from shore-based flak batteries should any crew inadvertently stray in that direction. A steady casualty rate would be borne during the offensive, although a reverse casualty rate in sunk and crippled vessels would make the campaign worth the effort in terms of MIA aircraft and their crews, tragic though this would prove.

For Valor 1

The above wording forms the simple inscription on Britain's supreme military award, the Victoria Cross. Two of the twenty-three airmen serving with Bomber Command—all but two based in the UK—were manning Stirlings, with neither surviving the event that earned them the medal. The first was F/Sgt. Rawdon Hume ("Hughie") Middleton from Australia, serving as a pilot with No. 149 Squadron. On November 28, 1942, he headed for Turin, but the mediocre altitude capability of the bomber nearly forced the raid to be aborted in view of the risk of failing to clear the Alpine mountain range.

Having barely managed to clear the geographic obstacle in BF372/OJ: H, he made three runs at minimum height over the target prior to bomb release. Flak struck home during the final run-up, with one blast around the cockpit seriously wounding Middleton, who had one eye destroyed as well as suffering chest and leg injuries. He passed out, but his second pilot, F/Sgt. Leslie Hyder, although also wounded, succeeded in pulling the aircraft out of its dive and releasing the bombs before turning for home. By then Middleton had regained consciousness and ordered his fellow pilot back to receive treatment.

He held his charge on course during the prolonged and physically punishing run up across France, but further flak damage was borne over the English Channel port of Boulogne. By the time the English coast was reached, the bomber was barely controllable, and Middleton gave the order to bail out. Five of the crew safely evacuated the dying machine; the pilot and the remaining duo had assisted him in holding the aircraft steady for their colleagues before preparing themselves to also jump as they directed the Stirling out toward the Channel. Tragically, the trio stood no chance when it abruptly went out of control and smashed into the waters. The award citation quoted Middleton's "fortitude and strength of will" in battling almost overwhelming physical odds and ensuring the bulk of his crew's survival at a personal cost. He lies in a graveyard at Beck Row, close to the squadron airfield of Mildenhall, and his gravestone reportedly bears the poignant statement "Thou knowest Lord the Secrets of our Heart."

That this is a Stirling assigned to No. 7 Squadron at Oakington is confirmed by the radically different hangar layout. Unlike the standard C- and D-type equivalents, which were rectangular in format, the J-type hangar seen here forms a continuous curve across its entire lateral span. Since the Lancaster, with its 102-foot wingspan, later displaced the Stirling, the fact appears to challenge the official reasoning limiting the latter's wingspan to below 100 feet.

The navigator's position was on the port side of the nose compartment and directly behind the pilot's seat. The reasonable size of the table that was aligned along the fuselage length enabled him to carry out his vital task in relative comfort. This crew member is plotting a course with the aid of a Dalton computer, a standard piece of RAF navigation equipment.

The photographer in an accompanying aircraft has caught a superbly detailed view of a Stirling's forward airframe. The outline of the nearside wing fuel tank covers is visible, as are the two aileron control cables. The exhaust stack position on the starboard engine cowlings denotes at least a late Mk. I Series I Stirling. The fixed radio mast, D/F loop, and small astrodome are standard features.

The very flat aspect of much of the East Anglian landscape where the Stirling squadrons of No. 3 Group were based is caught here. A duo of Mk. I Series III bombers are skimming the ground, with their silhouettes flitting along in close company. Low flying was not encouraged by the hierarchy, given the risk of either colliding with structures or having no time to recover should serious or terminal mechanical problems arise.

The ever-variable British weather patterns have cast a rather misty pall over Oakington. In the foreground is a No. 7 Squadron Stirling, while in the left background is a Wellington. The scenario unconsciously displays a "Changing of the Guard" image. The four-engine aircraft is the first of the three four-engine heavies taking up the bombing offensive from the original heavy trio: the Wellington along with the Whitley and Hampden designs, which served Bomber Command in this key role between 1939 and 1942.

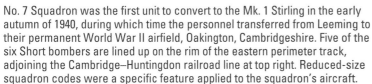

No. 7 Squadron was the first unit to convert to the Mk. 1 Stirling in the early autumn of 1940, during which time the personnel transferred from Leeming to their permanent World War II airfield, Oakington, Cambridgeshire. Five of the six Short bombers are lined up on the rim of the eastern perimeter track, adjoining the Cambridge–Huntingdon railroad line at top right. Reduced-size squadron codes were a specific feature applied to the squadron's aircraft.

An internal view looking forward from around the main entrance door provides confirmation this Stirling is a Mk. I Series I. The bulk of the retractable ventral turret is partially concealed by the three cylinders, which include the flare chute (*right*). The propensity for the turret to descend and snag the ground while taxiing, which added to the poor scanning capability for the gunner, saw its deletion at an early stage of production.

A Mk. I Series I or II, as denoted by the unbarbed exhaust pipes, provides a fine image of operational preparation. The AEC Bowser drawn up to the starboard wing is filling up the tanks between the motors, while a slave trailer provides oil to the port wing's engines. The large ground crew presence indicates a publicity shoot but does not detract from the sense of full readiness for an impending raid. The bomber's pristine condition suggests it is a recent arrival.

When the RAF commenced "Circus" operations over northern with a view to enticing JG 2's and JG 26's fighters into action, the bomber element under heavy escort was Blenheims. The Stirling was subsequently brought into the equation, as revealed by this somewhat blurred shot of a No. 15 Squadron Mk. I; several Hurricanes from the close escort are also seen. The tactic was rarely responded to directly by the Jagdwaffe pilots, however.

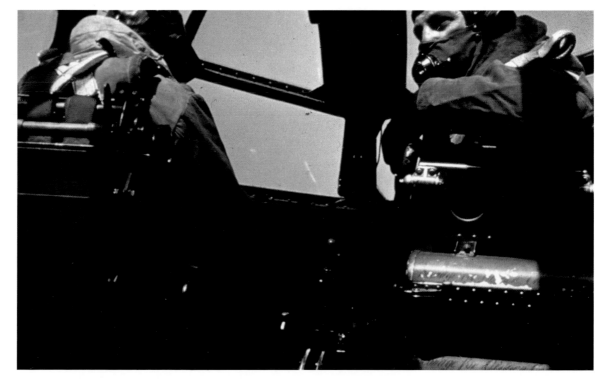

The original complement for a Stirling crew was set at eight, with the inclusion of two pilots—a logical act in view of the twin control facility. However, perceived future limitations on available numbers of aircrew volunteers as World War II advanced persuaded the Air Ministry to replace the second pilot with a flight engineer, who would monitor the bomber's engine performance and assist the pilot during takeoff and landing.

Mk. I N3641/MG: D rises steadily away from the runway at Oakington, the pilots trusting that there will no power lag or other mechanical problem that could prove disastrous at this minimal-altitude stage of takeoff. The aircraft is an early Series I, as confirmed by the spinner covers. Service with No. 7 Squadron was succeeded by assignment first to No. 26 Conversion Flight (CF) and then No. 15651 CU.

The displaying of RAF aircraft in civilian surroundings was indulged with a view toward raising morale, especially in blitzed cities and towns. Mk. I N6065 is suitably provided with a record of its success in handing out a reverse dose of punishment to Nazi Germany. The location is not stated but could be Belfast, where Shorts were producing the Stirling, and which was severely struck during the April–May 1941 period of the Blitz.

A Mk. I Stirling is tucked close in to the photographer's perch as he fires his camera from the rear cockpit, with the carburetor air intake frame (*left*) caught within the camera frame. The practice of leaving the tailwheels in an unretracted position appears to have been a regular practice while conducting nonoperational flights.

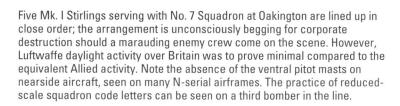

Five Mk. I Stirlings serving with No. 7 Squadron at Oakington are lined up in close order; the arrangement is unconsciously begging for corporate destruction should a marauding enemy crew come on the scene. However, Luftwaffe daylight activity over Britain was to prove minimal compared to the equivalent Allied activity. Note the absence of the ventral pitot masts on nearside aircraft, seen on many N-serial airframes. The practice of reduced-scale squadron code letters can be seen on a third bomber in the line.

Visits to World War II RAF units were indulged both by British and foreign royalty. In this instance, King Faisal of Iraq is snapped stepping out of Mk. I BF345. The bomber was originally assigned to No. 7 Squadron but was finally transferred to No. 1657 HCU, Stradishall. The thin white stripe indicates the aircraft's training status. The DANGER-headed wording warns individuals (with trainee aircrew undoubtedly in mind) to refrain from touching switches or levers—especially with reference to inadvertent landing-gear retraction!

Mk. I N3663 was another initial-production-run aircraft that is seen in the process of being loaded up for an op during its service with No. 7 Squadron. Cans of incendiaries in the foreground are supported by bomb trolleys behind bearing 500-pound bombs, the largest RAF medium-capacity missile capable of being stowed within the bomb bay. MG: H survived until the Berlin raid of August 2–3, 1941. Code letters are standard in size.

The servicing of any Stirling almost demanded ground crew personnel with a head for heights, if this view of a No. 7 Squadron Mk. I Series III is anything to go by. The multitier stands proved mandatory when attending to the Hercules engines; the airman on the left is courting disaster should he slip from the stand railing. The J-type hangar (*far left*) gives a clue to the squadron's Oakington location.

The tight formation flown by a trio of Mk. I Series III Stirlings is proceeding in a stately manner over the relatively flat expanses of East Anglia in which No. 3 Group was based. Although Bomber Command was largely indulging in nocturnal operations at this stage of World War II, a cohesive defensive firepower was available in this manner should a daylight operation have been called for. The single-letter code indicates an HCU or CU unit, however.

Mk. I Series III Bomber	
Wingspan	99 ft., 1 in.
Length	87 ft., 3 in.
Height	22 ft., 9 in.
Wing area	1,460 sq. ft.
Empty weight	46,900 lbs.
Maximum weight	59,400 (normal loaded) 70,000 lbs. (max. permissible)
Powerplant	Four 1,520 hp Bristol Hercules air-cooled radial engines
Armament	Eight .303 Browning machine guns in FN5 nose (two), FN7 or FN50 dorsal (two), and FN20A rear turret (four)
Performance	
Maximum speed	260 mph at 10,000 ft.
Service ceiling	15,000 ft.
Range	740 miles with 14,000 lbs., 1,930 miles with 5,000 lbs., 2,330 miles with 1,000 lbs.
Crew	8 (later 7)

A duo of Mk. I Stirling fuselages assume the rough appearance of whales as they await further assembly on the Austin Motors factory at Langbridge. A clue to their Mk. I status lies with the three small windows under the cockpit rim. These were reduced to two on the Mk. III, with the forward example bulged in design.

F/O Peter Boggis (*left*) and his crew pose for a one of a series of publicity pictures centered on N6086/LS: F "McRoberts Reply," which they are in the act of boarding. The Mk. I Stirling was dedicated to the three sons of Lady McRoberts, all of whom lost their lives in flying accidents, two on active service. Note the variations in flight suits and footwear. The aircraft was finally written off in an accident.

Whereas Boggis and some or all his crew survived their operational tour, their publicity charge was not so fortunate. A takeoff attempt from Dyce in northeastern Scotland went drastically wrong, with the result seen here. The fractured airframe lies in a snow-strewn area, with the port wing partially wrenched off; the heavy impact could so easily have escalated into an overall disintegration with fatal results for those on board.

Two bomb-laden trolleys already have the far-side weapons fitted with lifting frames. Cables lowered from the bomb bay will be attached, and each one winched up into position. A mechanic in the cockpit has the engines wound up to full power. OJ codes relate to No. 149 (East India) Squadron, based at Mildenhall starting in November 1941, followed by transfer to Lakenheath in April 1942.

The greatly extended height of the Stirling on the ground required the regular use of framed structures when attending to its maintenance. Even so, both mechanics attending to the starboard Hercules engines are balanced rather precariously in this picture. The pitot tubes are detached from their ventral metal sheaths in this case.

Mk. I N3669 enjoyed an unusual operational life. This commenced with No. 7 Squadron, followed by service with No. 26 Conversion Flight (CF). A return to operations with No. 15 Squadron culminated with transfer to No. 1 Air Armament School (AAS). The symbols behind the entrance hatch attest to the plane's survivability factor extending to sixty-seven ops. The reason for its current stripped-down condition is unknown.

An extended line of Mk. III Bostons assigned to No. 88 (Hong Kong) Squadron are being overflown by a solitary Stirling, whose tailwheels are not retracted. The airfield is probably Attlebridge, Norfolk (subsequent home for the 466th Bomb Group's B-24s), where the RAF unit converted to the Douglas bomber—a quantum leap in operational efficiency from their current Mk. IV Blenheims—around October 1941.

Mk. I N3663 was the twenty-ninth airframe among the first batch of one hundred turned out commencing in May 1940. It is seen being readied for a July 1941 op, with incendiary canisters and bomb trolleys arrayed under the bomb bay. The occasion is less than one month before the aircraft was declared FTR (failed to return) on a sortie to Berlin on August 8. The standard No. 7 Squadron letters indicate its early arrival at Oakington, these being later reduced in size during the year.

A photograph taken within the center fuselage of a Mk. I provides a closer view of the Nash and Thompson FN7A turret lower, the interior as well as the ladder providing access to and from the turret. The ammunition boxes are on either side, but the gunner's seat is not visible. The open main entrance door is seen between the ladder frames.

Three crew members are either assembled or, in the case of the individual on the right, are walking around this Mk. I of No. 149 Squadron. The wintry scene confirms a 1941–42 scenario, since the squadron converted to the design only in late 1941. There is no confirmation of whether the impending flight is operational or not, although the lack of depression on the main wheels suggests a light-laden bomber.

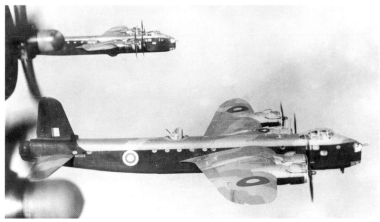

At first sight, the ground crew attending to the middle upper turret are involved in preparing their Stirling for an operation. A closer scan of the fuselage side reveals just a single aircraft letter; the absence of a squadron code indicates the aircraft is accordingly nonoperational and assigned to a training unit. The Stirling in the background is a Mk. I, Series I or II, both of whom lack the Series III's middle upper turret.

N6069 is a Mk. I Series III aircraft, as confirmed by the presence of the FN7 middle upper turret, and the fifth from a production batch commenced in September 1941. Its permanent assignment to No. 1651 Conversion Unit extended to July 29, 1942. That night, it was one of nearly a hundred OTU aircraft participating in a raid on Hamburg but was one of nine culled by the enemy defenses. Ventral pitot masts were a late application on N-serial Stirlings.

A sergeant who sports the VR shoulder flash, denoting his Volunteer Reserve status, is steadying a hoisting frame bearing a bomb prior to its being winched up into the bomb bay. This is most likely a publicity picture, since an airman of this rank would generally be supervising such an activity by those lower ranks under his supervision.

A pair of Mk. I Stirlings provide an overwhelming contrast with the No. 48 Squadron Avro Anson parked in the right background. The solid surface on the engine exhaust pipes confirms that the Stirling in the foreground is a Series I or II airframe; the equivalent fitting on the Series III featured a barbed exterior surface. The twin landing lamps in a Plexiglas cover outboard of the No. 1 engine are built into the wing, as opposed to the normal retractable location marginally below the leading edge.

R9304 was one of 150 Mk. I Stirlings produced between January 1942 and January 1943. Its status as one of the later airframes within the batch is confirmed by the FN50 middle upper turret displacing the original FN7A turret. Its then-current assignment to No. 1651 CU followed operations with No. 15 Squadron. The tailwheels are left in the lowered position during flight, which was often seen on the Mk. Is flown by CU and HCU aircraft.

The lifting frames for the individual quartet of bombs laden onto five trolleys are in the process of being fully fitted. They are aligned in front of a Mk. 1 Series II aircraft whose single code letter indicates a nonoperational bomber assigned to either an HCU or CU; in this instance the photo is part of a sequence shot at Waterbeach with No. 1651 HCU the unit concerned.

N3725/HA: D has the No. 4 engine fired up, but the likelihood that it is being prepared for a flight is belied by a seemingly innocuous but vital issue affecting the ventrally mounted pitot masts. The extended covers preventing foreign objects from entering the equipment are still in place, so any attempt to take off would almost certainly end in disaster, since the airspeed indicator would be registering zero. The No. 218 Squadron aircraft was destroyed in a crash returning from Wilhelmshaven on September 14–15, 1942.

N3751/BU: P lies in a largely intact condition within a flat stretch of the English countryside. The port stabilizer is almost wholly excised, whether by enemy action or impact with a solid object during the crash landing is unclear, while the propellers are buckled. The incident occurred following an op to Cologne on April 27–28, 1942, and the crew were fortunate to all survive the experience.

Three trolleys bearing bombs are aligned along the perimeter track in front of the No. 7 Sqdn. Mk. I within whose bomb bay they will be accommodated. Meanwhile, a fuel bowser's hoses are extended up to the starboard wing fuel tanks. Note the worn nose surface that confirms the poor adhesive quality of the Black RDM2 paint in current use.

The Stirling's overall fuselage outline as displayed by W7530 a No. 218 Sqdn. assignee was more angular compared to the Halifax or Lancaster. This bomber had originally flown with No. 149 Sqdn. after arriving at Mildenhall in early 1943 but its operational career was relatively short; on June 21, it was declared MIA off a sortie to the port of Enden.

A second picture of the No. 214 Squadron Mk. I depicts F/Sgt. F. Griggs, the darker color of uniform confirming his RAAF status, pointing to a bullet or flak fragment directly beneath the windshield; further proof of his nationality lies with the kangaroo artwork. Griggs later progressed to flying "Oboe" operations with No. 109 (PFF) Squadron along with his navigator, Sgt. P. O'Hara.

The background to this picture must be publicity based, since the crew would hardly be walking away from the Mk. I (a late-production Series I to judge by the switch from port to starboard of the exhaust pipe), whose Hercules engines are going at full bore. The flight clothing is standard for this stage of World War II, with footwear split between flying boots and leggings. Normal crew complement was either eight or seven when the second pilot was detached.

Mk. I W7446 was assigned to No. 7 Squadron in the early part of 1941 but bears the thin color stripe ahead of the fin denoting an aircraft assigned to training duties. However, the uniforms and flight clothing along with the casual strewing of equipment on the grass indicate that the airmen are regular operational personnel as opposed to trainees. This machine was written off on November 18, following a landing overshoot and landing-gear collapse.

An AEC fuel bowser is drawn up alongside a Stirling then serving with No. 1651 HCU at Waterbeach, Cambridgeshire. The anonymous Mk. I Series II airframe reveals little sign of operational deterioration to its surfaces and may well have been directly and permanently assigned to the secondary but vital duty of preparing trainee crews for Bomber Command operations.

W7446's seven-man crew are now assembled in full flight gear and ready to board their massive charge. The sad fact involving operational service with Bomber Command lies in that between three and four out of every seven of these volunteers would never complete their tours of duty, to end up either as fatal casualties or—if lucky—POWs.

A Mk. I Stirling from an anonymous squadron forms the background to a publicity picture that reveals the initial logistical and human support for each crew to ensure they can carry out their operational function. The technical personnel stand behind the crew or around their vehicles, while bomb trolleys are lined up in front. When clerks, cooks, and countless other support groups are added in, it adds up to a huge human pyramid of ground support.

The crew of LS:H/N3669 are photographed in front of the rear fuselage that shows twenty of the sixty-two sortie markings by the main entrance door. The Mk. I had an interesting operational career that commenced with No. 7 Sqdn. based at Oakington, prior to its transfer to No. 149 Sqdn. It survived to end its days with No. 1 Air Armament School (AAS). Airman on left is aircrew thanks to his collar-mounted emergency whistle but his tunic strangely bears no badge.

W7629/LS:J is photographed from the rear cockpit of an accompanying Stirling as it holds a close formation position. Bomber was another Austin Motors production airframe that reached No. 15 Sqdn. during early 1941. It served until the following October when a diversion into RAF Warboys resulted in a collapsed undercarriage caused by a severe swerve shortly after touching down.

The propensity for the two-stage Stirling landing gear to cast up its frailty is the most likely reason why a Mk. I Series III has ended up with its port wing hugging the airfield surface. Large inflatable bags will raise the aircraft back into a level attitude; the damage scale is likely to prove low enough for the bomber to resume operations following repair work.

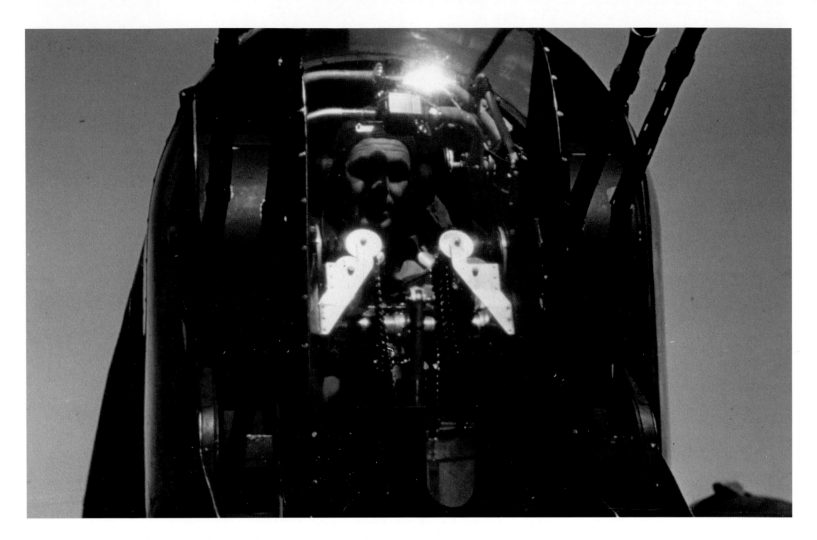

All three second-generation RAF bombers bore four-gun rear turrets, with the Stirling and Lancaster operating on the Frazer-Nash FN20 and FN120. Unfortunately, the striking power of the .303-caliber ammunition was no match for the Nachtjagd fighters' much-heavier bullet and cannon shell equivalent. Detachment of the central Plexiglas panel was often made with a view to gaining improved visual sighting of a bandit; even so, the experienced gunner opened fire only if given no other option.

The bulk of RAF aircraft servicing was conducted in the open, and the pleasant weather condition surrounding a No. 218 Squadron Mk. I was often the exception to the normal adverse conditions encountered by the ground crews. The need for tall stands from which to conduct activities such as engine maintenance is demonstrated, as is the risk of injury or death should anybody slip and fall from what was a height equivalent to the ceiling of a two-story house!

The role of the Women's Auxiliary Air Force (WAAF) was vital in providing comprehensive aircraft maintenance among their manifold duties. The several examples here are working on a Mk. I Series III assigned to No. 1651 HCU that is secured to the ground by cables; the landing-gear wheels are covered to guard against oil accretion seeping from the engines.

During 1941, the "circus" type of operation was laid on in a bid to draw Jagdwaffe units away from Russia and into sustained (and, it was hoped, costly) combat over France. This consisted of a small bomber force surrounded by a mass of RAF fighters as instanced here by a Stirling under close Hurricane escort. The tactic did not work, and the JG 2 and JG 26 *Gruppen* on permanent hand were more than able not only to fend off the attackers but inflict around a two-to-one kill/loss ratio in their favor.

No. 1651 Heavy Conversion Unit (HCU) was established at Waterbeach on January 2, 1942, with subsequent transfers to Wratting Common (November 1943) and Woolfox Lodge (November 1944). Two Mk. I Stirlings are taxiing out for takeoff; the type C1 markings confirm the photograph was taken at the second- or last-named airfield.

The original middle upper turret fitted to the Mk. I Stirling was provided by the distinctive egg-shaped FN7. However, this was displaced on later-production airframes by the FN50 turret, as seen on this aircraft, which provided enhanced all-around visual acuity. It is currently assigned to No. 1657 HCU, currently based at Stradishall, Suffolk.

By the summer of 1942, the Stirling was well entrenched within the ranks of Bomber Command. The scene at No. 218 Squadron's Downham Market location purports to show a bomber being prepared for an op. However, the absence of guns in the FN5 turret coupled with the ground personnel pulling the bomb trolley away from the aircraft appears to contradict this impression. The trolley accumulator, providing external engine start, is plugged in, so a nonoperational flight might be planned.

The pilot of this No. 7 Squadron Mk. I brought off a wheels-down landing near Gorinchem, Holland, on August 16, 1942, but the bomber suffered damage to the bomb aimer's compartment in the process, judging by the canvas wrapping around the front fuselage. Its airworthy condition would result in transfer to Rechlin, the Luftwaffe's research center. Two airmen (*left*) are preparing a webbed device to hold the canvas in place.

A photographer in an aircraft overflying the site where the Stirling force-landed has caught the bomber in its altered configuration. All RAF markings have been obliterated, and a Balkenkreuz is prominently displayed on the fuselage along with a fin-mounted Hakenkreuz. The destruction of the pitot masts depicted in the foregoing picture must have created a problem for the crew tasked with flying the aircraft; however, early-production Mk. I airframes were not so configured, so the problem likely never evolved.

The Stirling is depicted as it taxies out for takeoff. The camouflage pattern has been altered on the lower sides and undersides; in place of black, the Luftwaffe staff has applied a yellow substitute. The trapezoidal wing leading edge and extended pitot mast of the photographer's aircraft confirm its Ju 88 status; the aircraft will accompany the bomber to Rechlin, where its performance will be evaluated.

No. 15 Squadron, based at Mildenhall, Suffolk, was an early operator of the Stirling while based at Wyton between May 1940 and August 1942. The circumstances leading to a nose stand by an anonymous squadron flying Mk. I Series III planes is unclear, but the crew are arguably fortunate that their charge remained basically intact. The incident occurred shortly before a move to Bourn, Cambridgeshire, in August.

The sheer scale of the Stirling's airframe is encapsulated in this close-up of an anonymous example's forward fuselage. The crew member stationed by the forward cockpit frame appears minuscule by comparison. Barbed engine exhausts confirm this is a Series III variation. Note also the square light-color tape outline on the port wing, denoting the crew dinghy compartment. Wing surfaces are thoroughly stained by the twin effects of weathering and engine exhaust discharge.

Ridgewell in west Essex had originally been home for the Stirlings of No. 90 Squadron, prior to the unit decamping during May–June 1943, in favor of the 381st Bomb Group's B-17s. This latter-day Mk. I visitor to the USAAF airfield belongs to No. 1657 Conversion Unit (CU), stationed at nearby RAF Stradishall.

Mk. I N3725 HA: D was assigned to No. 218 Squadron at Marham during the winter of 1941–42. The Short Co. design's ever-massive format provides the background to the visible trio of trailers, holding incendiary cannisters to be loaded into the equally sizable bomb bay. The clear weather conditions in East Anglia provide no guarantee of similar patterns providing visual target access over the Continent.

A Mk. 1 Series I Stirling hovering bare feet above an airfield's grass surface presents an unconsciously daunting image to the photographer; he will be fortunate if the portside landing-gear wheel does not decapitate him, given the bomber's minimal height and head-on alignment with this individual. Photo angle allows a clear view of the original outer location of the engine exhaust pipes, and twin tailwheel fitting peculiar to the design.

The month is October in 1944, as backed up by the leafless treeline, at which stage of World War II the Mk. I had long been withdrawn from frontline service and in numerous cases reassigned to CU or HCU service. Two airmen pose on the outer starboard wing, with a third attending to the No. 4 engine cowling.

F/Sgt. Leslie Hyder (copilot) is recovering from wounds received on November 22–23, 1942, over Turin. The No. 15 Squadron Mk. I was flak-stricken, and F/Sgt H. M. Middleton (RAAF) was critically injured. Despite this, he and Hyder attained England's Channel coast before being abandoned; Middleton and two others did not survive, but the pilot's extreme gallantry was subsequently recognized by the award of the Victoria Cross, the nation's highest military decoration.

A Mk. I Stirling attached to No. 1651 HCU is about to have the port-outer wing tank or tanks replenished from the AEC Bowser parked in front. Three snakelike hose lengths stretch upward, but the airman appears to have just one on hand. The obvious steep wing camber would create a hazardous platform in wet or icy conditions. Unit code letters BS (ironically indicating "bulls**t" to the average "erk"—RAF slang for ground crew) are seen on aircraft behind.

A lineup of Bomber Command's new generation of four-engine designs is fronted on the left by a Mk. I Stirling, with a Mk. II Halifax nearby and what looks like the nose of a Lancaster farther on. The occasion was an official inspection laid on for the prime minister. Churchill is in the center, followed by the usual retinue of service and civilian senior staff.

A retraction test is being conducted on a Stirling's port landing gear. The lower half is in the process of folding into a horizontal position, after which the entire unit will rise vertically into the engine nacelle. The large wheel with its treadless rubber surface equals the height of the three airmen. The need for two hinge points made for a less sturdy structure compared to normal single-hinge layouts and was therefore more prone to failure should a hard landing be made.

The open spaces around St. Paul's Cathedral, formerly occupied by buildings destroyed by the Luftwaffe on December 29, 1940, provide a convenient location for a Mk. I Stirling now under public scrutiny. Such aircraft were used for raising funds donated by Britain's citizens and intended to go toward the war effort, as well as displaying the nation's resolve to hammer the enemy's industrial resources into oblivion in this case through their burgeoning production.

What is a Stirling Mk. I Series III is confirmed by the barbed flame-damping exhausts. The ground crew numbers indicate a publicity scenario, with the airman on the No. 3 propeller risking injury or worse should he slip from his precarious perch. The original aircraft letter is crudely deleted, while a red letter R is the sole identification for what is an HCU or similar training unit (no Bomber Command squadron operating Stirlings featured R in its code letters).

A close-up of the largest bomb capable of being loaded into a No. 218 Squadron Stirling's bomb bay is arrayed on its trolley. The 2,000-pound weapon was an aerodynamic "blunt instrument" since it was incapable of accurate aiming. Instead, its explosive force was intended to open up structures to facilitate the accompanying incendiary bomb ignition. |It was the precursor to the even more basic 4,000-pound "Cookie" borne by the Halifax and Lancaster, with their single-cell bomb-bay layout.

Mk. I N3667/LS: T is seen in late 1941, albeit not at its normal squadron location of Wyton. It was probably functioning in Exercise Trinity, a series of electronic experiments in blind bombing that would culminate with the very effective "Oboe" target-marking system. The presence of a Spitfire and Defiant night fighter lends credence to the assumption, with other pictures showing a Boston. The aircraft was written off soon after, following a crash returning from Nuremberg on October 12.

The photographer has concentrated his lens on the starboard pair of Hercules engines as his aircraft proceeds in the company of a second Mk. I. as both skirt a solid cumulonimbus cloud formation. The distinctive carburetor air intake on the cowling top would give way to an extended, more shallow, and more aerodynamic profile on the subsequent Stirling variants from the Mk. III onward.

Mk. I W7459 had a very varied career; it served with Nos. 149, 218, and 214 Squadrons but in between these operational spells was assigned to the conversion flights of the second and third quoted unit, as well as two spells with No. 1651 CU. It was finally SOC on July 19, 1945. The photo shows up the poor adhesive quality of the RDM2 paint and the aircraft's critical vulnerability to assault from a ventral angle.

A line of Stirling fuselages at one of the Short Co. production plants are paralleled by pairs of wings intended for attachment to individual examples. The angle of the wings clearly reveals the apertures into which the fuel tanks allotted to each wing will be inserted. The FN7 dorsal turret on the near-side fuselage airframe confirms this is a Mk. I production line.

A Mk. I Stirling forms the backcloth to a quartet of overalls-clothed and toolkit-bearing members of the Womens' Auxiliary Air Force (WAAF), who will apply their skills to the waiting bomber. These service members provided a valuable asset to the RAF as they undertook a similar range of technical skills to their male counterparts during World War II.

The retention of a production Stirling in a horizontal configuration provides the two staff members with an arguably safer working environment, compared to when the bomber is raised up onto its stalky undercarriage to leave a dangerously high and angled working platform. The undercarriage is in position, ready for mounting into the engine nacelles whenever final assembly is launched.

The juxtapositioning of Bomber Command and 8th Air Force airfields across the length and breadth of East Anglia regularly resulted in aircraft landing on foreign soil. In this case the airman serving on an anonymous American base is walking away from a Mk. I Stirling assigned to No. 214 Squadron. The FN50 dorsal turret indicates a late-production airframe; the type C1 markings were introduced from mid-1942 onward.

A Mk. I Series III Stirling has the starboard inner engine at full power, judging by the total absence of the propeller's presence. The crew member facing the bomber is wearing full flight gear, including a fur-lined jacket and Mae West life vest as well as the original one-piece flying boots. Picture taken at Mildenhall or Lakenheath, where No. 149 Squadron served during its allocation of Mk. I Stirlings.

What is almost certainly a 2,000-pound bomb, to judge by the presence of the supporting incendiary containers, is commencing its hoist into a bomb bay of a No. 7 Squadron Mk. I. The trolley bearing a companion weapon is being aligned with the adjacent bomb cell by the pair of armorers.

A directly lateral view of a Mk. I's starboard wing from the cockpit demonstrates how dangerous the surface could prove to be to the ground crew working atop. It would be all too easy to lose one's footing in the wet conditions or with frost or snow coating the aircraft; a descent from nearly 16 feet onto the ground would witness any individual lucky to at least survive with broken limbs.

Two members of a German military unit are posed in front of the shattered rear fuselage of a Stirling. The ragged edges directly behind the door suggest either a very heavy crash landing or, alternately, that the bomber may well have descended intact and is being cut up for salvage. Code letters denote a No. 149 Squadron machine.

A bellied-in Mk. I lies in the vicinity of Ridgewell, home for the B-17s of the 381st Bomb Group. The aircraft, belonging to No. 1657 HCU, has survived the experience and remains in largely intact form, demonstrating its sturdy construction. Whether it will be restored to flight condition cannot be confirmed, however.

No. 1657HCU was created at Stradishall in October 1941, having absorbed the Conversion Flight (CF) of Nos. 7, 101, 149, and 218 Sqdns. The Mk. I manoeuvring along the 50 feet wide perimeter track whose limited width gave little margin for error should the pilot not maintain correct position, bears the code letters XT allotted to the HCU, along with aircraft letter M.

A more fortunate companion Mk. I from the same unit flies in close company of the photographer's aircraft. The tendency to leave the tailwheels in unretracted mode appears to have been a regular feature on this HCU.

The picture of a Stirling flying at low level, with a Wellington squatting on its dispersal in the left background, has an operationally symbolic aspect to it. The preeminence of the "Wimpy" along with the Whitley and Hampden in the initial stages of the bombing offensive would now give way to the four-engine contemporary aloft as it took over the mantle in concert with the Halifax and Lancaster as the Third Reich absorbed an ever-increasing weight of destructive effect.

(THE SHORT STIRLING Four 1,600 h.p. Bristol Hercules motors, H.D. Hydromatic airscrews)

A. Gunner's seat and canvas screen.
B. Parachute stowage.
C. Emergency hatch.
D. Recognition lights.
E. Stairway.
F. Dual controls.
G. Oxygen stowage.
H. Navigator's chart table.
J. Warm air conduit.
K. Gallay steam-air heater.

L. Air inlet to Gallay heater.
M. Oil cooler inlets.
N. Steam circuit (exhaust to Gallay heater).
P. Radio operator's compartment.
Q. Fresh water tank.
R. Water bottles.
S. Astro hatch.
T. D.F. loop.
U. Oxygen bottles.
V. Anti-icer fluid tank (for slinger-rings).
W. Fuel equaliser valve.
X. Electric motor flap drive.

Y. Worm for raising and lowering under-carriage.
Z. Trunnion support for worm (Y).
a. Two seats on ladder leading to midships turret.
b. Flares.
d. Elsan lavatory.
e. Tail wheel retracting gear (electric and hand).
f. Built-in mass balance.
g. Sliding door (bulkhead for conserving warm cabin air).

h. Engineer's compartment. (Also in front of spar.) Note wing reinforcing.
k. Armoured bulkhead (pilot's compartment).
m. Bunk.
n. Trailing aerial fairlead.
p. Bomb doors and operating mechanism.

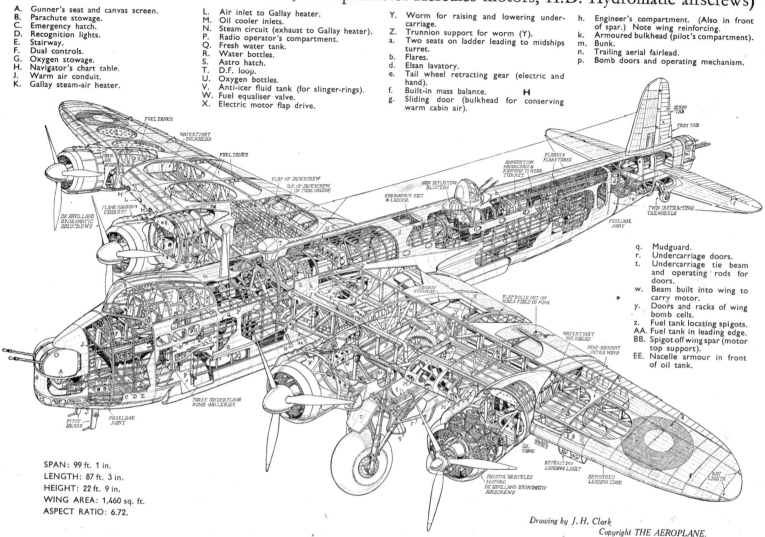

SPAN: 99 ft. 1 in.
LENGTH: 87 ft. 3 in.
HEIGHT: 22 ft. 9 in.
WING AREA: 1,460 sq. ft.
ASPECT RATIO: 6.72.

q. Mudguard.
r. Undercarriage doors.
t. Undercarriage tie beam and operating rods for doors.
w. Beam built into wing to carry motor.
y. Doors and racks of wing bomb cells.
z. Fuel tank locating spigots.
AA. Fuel tank in leading edge.
BB. Spigot off wing spar (motor top support).
EE. Nacelle armour in front of oil tank.

Drawing by J. H. Clark
Copyright THE AEROPLANE.

A full view of the Mk. I Stirling with the interior exposed provides a sound insight into the overall layout. An alphabetic list of the various basic equipment and fittings accompanies the diagram.

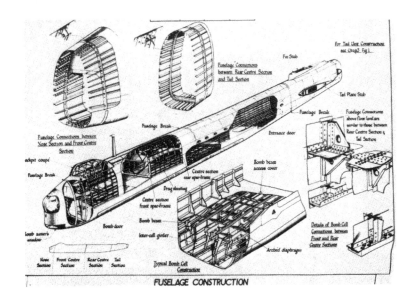

FUSELAGE CONSTRUCTION

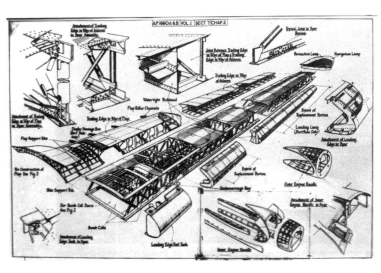

A closer view of the fuselage reveals the internal frame structure around where the wings match up, as well as the joining points for the four fuselage subsections.

An exploded view of the Stirling's wing is displayed in full, with separate leading-edge, central, and trailing-edge segments outlined, along with wingtip and engine nacelles.

Seven airmen under training are fully geared up and ready to board Mk. I W7459 operating with No. 1657 Heavy Conversion Unit (HCU). The bomber was built by Austin Motors, a subcontracted company, in early 1941and was operational with Nos. 149 and 7 Sqdns. prior to being withdrawn to serve in the secondary albeit key role of providing the final stage for a crew to graduation and assignment to a front-line unit.

In what is likely a publicity picture, an intelligence officer is talking to six members of a Mk. I Stirling crew. However, the aircraft is not in frontline service but is assigned to a training unit judging by the single aircraft letter code. Both inboard Hercules engines have left their exhaust staining on the wing surfaces compared to the outboard pair.

CHAPTER 3

Mk. II

Mk. I N3711 was selected as the second out of four airframes to be converted to the US power source, the Wright Cyclone, but only N3657 accompanied this machine to Boscombe Down for evaluation tests during March 1942, where it is photographed. No substantial performance advance was experienced, and the project was duly canceled.

The availability of overseas production facilities was a critical factor in adding to Britain's stocks of military hardware, with aircraft a prominent example. The rationale behind this was twofold. First, the countries concerned, Canada and Australia, were basically immune from aerial assault that could adversely affect supplies of aircraft. Second, the immunity simply added to available stocks of aircraft with which to supplement UK production.

Canada, being geographically closer at hand in terms of overall distance from Britain, probably dictated its initial selection. In the case of the Stirling, a secondary consideration was the overwhelming industrial resources available within the United States, which saw focus on the choice of engine power. The Wright Co. was requested, and a contract drawn up, to provide their radial 1,600 hp Cyclone R-2600-A5BB; the power plant's overall efficiency was already proven thanks to its application to the B-17 Fortress.

During late 1941, four Mk. I airframes were converted to the Cyclone power plant at Rochester, two of which (N3657 and 3711) were fully evaluated. The sole external difference related to the engine cowlings; the original carburetor air intakes were deleted and replaced with a slimmer version mounted at the front; a second alteration, involving the exhaust stacks, witnessed their switch from starboard to a lower-port location. The 100 hp boost in output vis-à-vis the Hercules XI apart, no distinct improvement in overall performance, was experienced, and by early 1942 the decision was taken to cancel the project. Parallel plans for Lancaster and Mosquito Canadian production would fare far better, while Merlin production by the Packard Co. would supplement Rolls-Royce stocks for both designs.

A rear view of one of the four aircraft refitted with the Wright Cyclone engine picks out the absence of the carburetor air intakes, which are standard on the Hercules cowling frames. Five dark lines on the Gouge flap are the roller rails that direct its deployment and retraction. Photo angle also shows how the outboard engine is mounted centrally along the wing leading edge compared to its inner partner, whose top surface barely protrudes above the wing surface.

CHAPTER 4
Mk. III

What was destined to be the majority-production variant out of the 2,374 overall figure of Stirling airframes was first mooted around the same time as the Mk. II's cancellation. The one change expected to improve performance lay with the new Hercules XVI, rated at 1,650 hp. The engine cowlings were modified to accommodate a carburetor air intake with an extended and flatter profile, and with the oil cooler switched from the wing leading edge to the cowling underside and enclosed within a circular-shaped cover placed directly behind the cowling gills. Ice guards and air cleaners were added within the front, and the cooling element was fitted with thermostatically controlled shutters.

There were external alterations to the fuselage, the obvious one affecting the middle upper gun location. In place of the egg-shaped FN7, the circular pattern FN50 was applied, the replacement having already featured on late production Mk. Is. The all-around visual Plexiglas shape was an advance on its predecessor, which had a blanked-off metal rear hindering all-around scrutiny for the gunner, a key requirement in picking out hostile aircraft. The number of fuselage windows was reduced to groups of three and four (sometimes five) on both sides; the forward trios, which were a mix of bulged and flat Plexiglas, featured two below the cockpit sill and one ahead of the wing leading edge, and the rear groupings stretched back from a point in line with the main wing spar.

Mk. I R9309 was selected as the prototype and took to the air in its adapted format at Rochester, to be followed by official evaluation at Boscombe Down in June 1942. The test cast up an initial climb rate of 500 fpm to 12,000 feet, after which a further ten minutes was required to attain 15,000 feet; however, the latter rate of 300 fpm was almost double that for the Mk. I. Maximum speed of 270 mph occurred at 14,000 feet. The maximum range of 2,010 miles allowed for a marginal load of 3,500 pounds, with the maximum load of 14,000 pounds conversely limiting range to less than one-third, a factor that seriously intruded on the bomber's ability to strike targets anywhere beyond Germany's western boundaries. In any event, the range/load statistics would land up in between these extremes, and the Stirling would add to RAF Bomber Command's ability to punish the Third Reich homeland across its entire interior, although not sustaining the function beyond November 1943.

Operations

The Mk. III commenced operations during the winter of 1942–43, a time spell coinciding with the fortunes of Bomber Command steadily ascending from its late 1941 nadir to an ultimate crescendo of success. The bomber stream concept was by now firmly entrenched in practice and was being paralleled by distinct advances in navigational systems and target marking. The buildup in Mk. III numbers witnessed a converse withdrawal from bombing operations of the Mk. I, but not its practical use. A switch to training duties with the manifold HCU and CU (heavy conversion unit and conversion unit) establishments would witness a regular service in this role right up to 1945.

Two armament provisions on the Mk. III were mooted at this stage. The first involved the installation of the FN64 ventral turret, but the venture never advanced beyond the point of discussion. As events dictated the introduction of the H2S, sets located in the same area behind the bomb bay negated the proposal, as well as the alternative of a single .303. The second involved the introduction of the FN82 in place of the FN20A. The gunners would have welcomed the superior striking power of the twin .50-caliber machine guns compared to the FN20's quartet of .303 weapons, but center-of-gravity problems when experimenting

The Mk. III Stirling first appeared on operations during the winter of 1942–43. Apart from the switch to the Hercules XVI engine, rated at 1,650 hp, it bore an extended carburetor air-intake frame. In addition, it featured a FN50 middle upper turret in place of the Mk. I's FN7; both changes are depicted on a still-anonymous bomber.

with the FN82 again saw the scheme canceled (a more personal advantage for the gunners would have been the ability to wear their parachute packs due to the extra turret dimensions, a feat impossible to achieve in the space-inhibited FN20A). One amendment involved the pitot masts, which were reduced from two to a single unit.

The prospects of surviving a ditching had hitherto seen the Stirling crews forced to depend on the single large J-type dinghy contained in the port wing. Now, the spacious interior was utilized with several individual K-type dinghies, located in stowage frames within immediate reach of each crew member—a distinct advantage over the Lancaster and Halifax, whose interiors reportedly did not provide the necessary space for a similar disposition.

No. 3 Group's Stirling crews were to play a regular part in what were termed the three battles conducted under ACM Harris's orders. The first concerned a prolonged battering of the Ruhr industrial zone as its epicenter, along with other targets in central Europe, between March 5–6 and July. The second battle involved a single entity in the form of the city of Hamburg, which was pounded on four nights between July 24–25 and August 2–3. Finally came the Battle of Berlin, spread between August 1943 and March 1944.

The Stirling was clearly demonstrating its operational limitations by the onset of the latter battle. Casualty rates were noticeably greater even within the overall hammering that Bomber Command was then suffering at the hands of the Nachtjagd and flak defensive screen. As the range of briefed targets began to stretch ever farther afield and the average operation's flight time was extended accordingly, the Short design's ability to bear a worthwhile bomb / incendiary load would tend to be degraded, to the extent that a figure of 3,000 or 4,000 pounds was being realized as 1943 was drawing to a close.

The resultant minimal return in terms of contributing to the overall offensive's effect, coupled to the growing loss percentage (109 crews or 6.4 percent between August and mid-November), finally persuaded Harris that the Stirling squadrons should be deleted from the Bomber Command's establishment. On November 22–23, the forty-five crews returning out of fifty dispatched by No. 3 Group were unaware that never again would their charges participate directly in a Bomber Command strike. The operational record of the Mk. III would not now expire, however; the functions of minelaying and dropping personnel and supplies to Resistance groups within Occupied Europe would absorb the attention of several of the squadrons withdrawn from Harris's Command.

Mk. III BF480/HA:I is seen after swerving on landing at Downham Market as it completed the sortie to Bochum in Germany. The No. 1 engine lies detached with the starboard-outer wing completely excised; both the crew and personnel in the Watch Office were fortunate that the bomber's momentum was spent barely short of impacting with the building. Incident occurred on May 14, 1943, during the Battle of the Ruhr.

A figure of 1,047 Mk. III Stirling airframes would be produced, initially prosecuting the bombing offensive up to November 1943, after which active operations involving minelaying and supporting the SOE in delivering supplies to the Resistance movements would continue until the European conflict's conclusion. Here, a Mk. III thunders low over a fellow Mk. III, with both ready to advance from this production source at either the Rochester, Belfast, or Austin Motors, Longbridge factories.

The unsung heroes behind the frontline aircrew within Bomber Command were the civilian personnel who flight-tested the factory-completed aircraft. Their expertise ensured that the aircraft were in all respects ready to provide those pursuing their operational existence with the best possible chance of bringing their charges back safely.

For Valor 2

The second of the Victoria Cross (VC) awards to Bomber Command aircrew operating on the Stirling involved a scenario containing two common elements, the first being the target selected—Turin in northern Italy. In addition, neither F/Sgt. Middleton nor F/Sgt. Louis Aaron would survive the incidents. However, whereas the former airman's death would arise from direct enemy assault, Aaron's loss would emerge from a friendly-fire source.

The No. 218 Squadron Mk. III EF452/HA: O was heading out on August 12–13, 1943, when disaster struck. The constant danger of an air gunner mistaking another bomber for a hostile aircraft was sadly demonstrated as the target loomed. The burst of fire riddled the forward fuselage, wounding several crew members and killing the navigator. The pilot, F/Sgt. Louis Aaron, was struck by a bullet that excised part of his face and shattered his jaw; his sight was also affected, and his right arm was paralyzed.

Dosed with morphia, he was removed, and the bomb aimer and flight engineer undertook the daunting task of heading for North Africa, hundreds of miles distant, and without the benefit of a navigator's crucial services. The duo battled on and finally reached Tunisia and Bone airfield. Aaron had regained consciousness by then and insisted on taking his seat for the landing. His overall condition prevented him from operating the controls, so he was again replaced either by Sgt. T. Guy (WOP) or Sgt. M. Mitcham (BA); he could not speak but, by means of written notes, provided advice on how to make a safe approach. The bomber was finally brought down safely, albeit on its belly, following the fifth approach effort.

Aaron was extracted and taken to a hospital, his lease on life extended for a mere nine hours. His colleagues believed he might have survived had he remained at rest instead of attempting to regain his position. The subsequent announcement of the VC on November 5 concluded by reflecting on "the appalling conditions despite which he showed the greatest qualities of courage, determination and leadership; although wounded and dying, he set an example of devotion to duty that has seldom been equalled and never surpassed." The two involuntary pilots were awarded the Distinguished Flying Medal.

Mk. III EF452/HA: O displays no visible external evidence of the carnage wrought among several crew members, including the pilot, F/Sgt. Louis Aaron, during the op to Turin on August 12–13, 1943. The wounds, which proved ultimately fatal after the bomber received "friendly fire" from another aircraft, and his gallantry in keeping the aircraft aloft before crash-landing in North Africa later earned him the Victoria Cross, Britain's supreme military award.

An anonymous Mk. III Stirling squats upon its dispersal area as an AEC fuel bowser positioned in front of the starboard wing is replenishing the wing tanks. The surrounding country landscape provides a sharp contrast in tranquillity to the aerial implement of war in its midst.

A Stirling assigned to No. 15 Sqdn. as seemingly confirmed by the LS letters on the bomb-trolley side is being loaded with a mix of 250-lb. bombs along with a single cylindrical 2,000-lb. blast weapon. The bomb attached to its crutch-frame and being hoisted into the bomb bay bears what seems to be a mass of stickers but what these relate to is unclear, although their message to Hitler and his regime would hardly be generous!

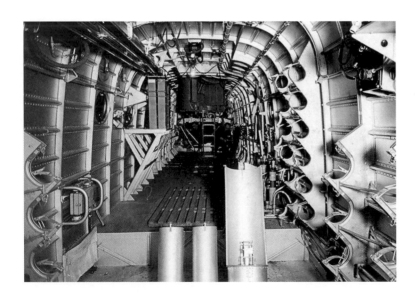

The generous internal proportions of the bomber were further exemplified by this photograph of the fuselage center section. The middle upper turret's bulk is evident, with the access ladder attached to the base. What looks like ammunition boxes are stowed on a shelf with angled support frames. The flare chute appears to be the one with an extended upper portion down which to slide each flare.

Stirling production reached a final figure of 2,374 airframes, and this picture reveals the various stages of construction. A single example with wings attached (*left background*) contrasts with the row of fuselages in the foreground. Note the trio of FN gun turrets in the center front. The unit directly behind the FN5 nose turret is an FN50 mid-upper that displaced the FN7 applied to the Mk. I (including later-production airframes) and became a standard fitting on the Mk. III.

H2S

The introduction of "Gee" in 1941, which allowed navigators to plot an accurate course, albeit not beyond the Earth's curvature—a limitation that still encompassed the Ruhr industrial complex—was followed by H2S and "Oboe" in early 1943. The former electronic device was a plan-position indicator whose rotating frame cast up a rudimentary light/dark impression on the set screens of the ground passing beneath the bomber, the shades relating to solid ground—towns showing up as brighter "blobs"—and water stretches. Its presence was of double benefit to the navigator's ability both to navigate and pick out a briefed target zone. What was confident theory would prove to be far from guaranteed in practice, however. The equipment's installation was accordingly initially focused on No. 8 (PFF) Group, with Nos. 7 and 35 Squadrons having their Stirling and Halifax establishment equipped. The scanner equipment was mounted behind the bomb bay and enclosed in a "teardrop" cover.

The sets made their operational debut on January 30–31, over Hamburg, but the results were disappointing. Although the accuracy factor would improve, there would be regular occasions when the interpretation by the navigators of the screen returns proved to be faulty, a situation for the PFF crews that would result in their markers going astray and inevitably lead to targets being marginally struck or left totally unaffected. An even worse reverse was suffered only two nights later, when Mk. I Stirling R9264 was lost over Cologne. The resultant crash still left enough of the H2S set capable of salvage and dispatch to the electronics manufacturer Telefunken. The immediate result was the enemy's ability to test the set and then to develop an aerial countermeasure.

This took the form of Naxos, which was installed in the Nachtjagd fighters from late November onward, and whose radar operators (*Bordfunker*) could pick up the H2S emissions and direct their pilots into an attacking position. It is ironic and at least marginally fortunate that the Stirling's presence within the Bomber Command had concluded around the same time; otherwise it would have shared in the figure of bombers culled in this fashion. However, the presence of the Lichtenstein radar sets over the previous year or so, along with the *schräge-Musik* upward-firing cannon coming on stream starting in August, had nevertheless critically affected the ranks of all three heavy-bomber designs within the bomber stream, to an extent that the offensive's very continuance was in doubt.

No. 100 (RCM) Group

Although the Stirling was gone from the bombing offensive in direct terms by late 1943, this did not mean its future conduct was totally directed elsewhere. In fact, it would be provided with an alternative role in the campaign, albeit with a more indirect if equally vital part in thwarting the enemy's ability to provide an effective defensive network. The development of electronic "magic" devices with which to carry out such deceptive measures had led to the creation of No. 100 (Radio Countermeasures) Group over the 1943–44 period of operations.

Nos. 171 and 199 Squadrons were assigned the specific duty of carrying out operations to jam the aerial and ground radar signals via the use of "Mandrel." The sets cast up blinding emissions, behind which the attacking bombers were invisible until they broke into the clear. Up to mid-1944, the Main Force formation had constituted a single stream, but from then on, the practice would be for several subforces to be regularly dispatched to widely spread targets on a single operation, with a view to splitting the Nachtjagd response.

The "Mandrel" sets were located on the starboard center of the fuselage, and a series of stick aerials mounted in ventral positions, mainly along the length of the bomb bay, were the conduits for the jamming-signal emissions. A chute was fitted ahead of the Lorenz beam approach aerial, through which "Window" strips were fed to further jam enemy electronic transmissions. The first operation on June 5, in connection with Overlord, did have the anticipated deleterious effect on the defensive network, but the powerful signals similarly disrupted the Allies' own network. Fortunately, all future operations commenced over the North Sea and advanced eastward in concert with the Allied armies' advances on the Continent.

Not only did the presence of "Mandrel" among the several electronic devices in use conceal genuine bomber forces; on occasions the "Mandrel" jamming would conceal nothing at all. Since the Luftwaffe staff could not confirm if the cover was shielding a feint, the dispatch of its night fighters toward the covered zone would prove fruitless as well as wasting ever-shrinking fuel reserves as the German oil industry was hammered into a state of ruin.

Four Mk. III Stirlings are lined up on the grass verges of Mildenhall, where No. 15 Squadron were then based, on what is a hot day in mid-1943, to judge by the airmen on the right. The bombers are being readied to receive their loads of incendiary containers. These inflammable as opposed to explosive missiles tended to be the regular content for the Short Co. design during the final months of its service with Bomber Command, when the ever-longer distances to be flown restricted its overall load capacity.

Mk III Bomber	
Wingspan	99 ft., 1 in.
Length	87 ft., 3 in.
Height	22 ft., 9 in.
Wing area	1,460 sq. ft.
Empty weight	46,900 lbs.
Maximum weight	70,000 lbs.
Powerplant	Four 1,650 hp Bristol Hercules Mk. XVI air-cooled radial engines
Armament	Eight .303 Browning machine guns in FN5 nose (two), FN50 dorsal (two), and FN20 (rear) gun turrets

Another photograph of a Stirling production line picks out what could be either a late-production Mk. I or a standard Mk. III fuselage. The surround for the middle-upper turret covering the taboo track, preventing a gunner from inadvertently firing into the airframe, was pertinent to the FN50 that displaced the original FN7 unit on the Mk. I, as stated above.

Ops are on and a row of Stirlings from an anonymous squadron await the arrival of those who will entrust their lives to the efficient function of the airborne machines. The Stirling would do its best to match this basic requirement in the face of its limitations, with inferior maximum altitude a sadly prominent inhibitor.

The seven totally or partially visible ground crew struggling with the portside landing-gear wheel of a Stirling that outsizes all of them are doing so with what appears to be the OJ codes on a No. 149 Squadron bomber. The detail of the wheel's support frame is fully displayed, including the large panel in between the main support struts. The wheel surface bears no tread lines.

An interior view of the rear fuselage depicts what was a physical relief facility, but one rarely utilized. It is the Elsan chemical toilet, the bin-shaped unit in the lower left. Its position so far distant from the bulk of the crew positions, coupled with the inevitable risk of instant frost bite should anyone risk sitting on its surface, rendered it useless in practice. Note the forward section of the solid transverse beam, linking the horizontal stabilizers, and the overhead ammunition feed racks for the rear turret.

Directly behind the main entrance door on the right side of the fuselage can be found the location for the flare stowage racks, four of which are depicted with the large fin-supported missiles in place. The flare chute down which they are released is seen on the left-hand side of the photograph.

SOE Operations

In 1940, Winston Churchill was wholeheartedly behind the creation of resistance movements within Nazi-occupied Europe, whose members would commit acts of sabotage to hinder the German military and economic structures. In the prime minister's ever-eloquent language, these secretive warriors would "set Europe ablaze." The absence of arms and support equipment with which to commence and subsequently sustain these activities would of necessity have to be delivered by air, a duty allotted to the Special Operations Executive (SOE).

The initial period of air operations by what were titled Special Duties (SD) operations involved Lysander and Whitley squadrons, but by 1943–44 the enhanced range and load-bearing capability of the Stirling witnessed the role being taken up after its displacement from the bombing offensive. As with minelaying operations, the crews had to fly at minimal altitudes to ensure precise delivery of the supplies. This placed an intense pressure on the pilot to avoid inadvertent contact with the topography or man-made obstacles, and even more so the navigator or bomb aimer, the latter airman having recourse to map reading to and from what were often several-hundred-mile-distant sites, with France as a prime example—a precise and exhausting task for these specialists within each crew.

Avoiding defensive locations was another constant and unpredictable hazard, since these could easily intrude on the aircraft's flight path and result in frantic evasive action. Given these manifold problems, it was inevitable that casualties would be incurred, but the loss scale proved to be borne at a reasonable level throughout the conflict. The effectiveness of the assaults was later regarded by Gen. Dwight D. Eisenhower as playing a salient part in the initial success of D-day by causing indecision and vital delay in the German initial response to the invasion.

P/O Peter Buck (*left*) inspects the severe damage to the rear turret and rudder base to the No. 75 (RBZAF) Squadron Mk. III operating out of Mepal; whether flak gunners or a Nachtjagd fighter inflicted the punishment is unclear, but the gunner would have been extremely fortunate to emerge alive from the action. The central Plexiglas panel on the turret has been detached for increased visibility.

The trio of Mk. III Stirlings assigned to No. 90 Squadron is dispersed on what was formerly their domain of Ridgewell in Essex but was by now reallocated to the US VIII Bomber Command and occupied by the B-17-equipped 381BG. In fact, the last Stirling did not depart for its new airfield at nearby Wratting Common until June, several weeks following its transatlantic contemporary's arrival.

Mildenhall's latest casualty on April 20–21, 1943, involved No. 15 Squadron's Mk. III BF476, which was the twenty-second airframe from the initial production batch of this variant. The forward fuselage and inner-wing sections are consumed by fire, while the middle upper turret Plexiglas and entire rear turret are excised. The aircraft was one of eight examples out of an eighty-six-strong Stirling force bombing Rostock that ended up MIA; the crew's fate is unknown.

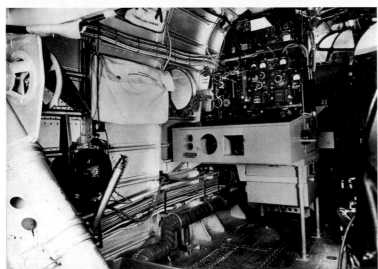

The radio operator's position was on the port side but was normally farther back behind the armored bulkhead located at the rear of the cockpit frame. His radio equipment and desk are aligned at right angles to the fuselage length. The armored bulkhead normally separating the equipment from the pilot's compartment ahead is absent, an indication that this is an airframe being assembled on the production-line circular frame (*lower left*) that contains the trailing aerial.

The noticeable dimensions of a Stirling compared to any of the other four RAF or USAAF four-engine contemporaries are illustrated by a Mk. III seen at Bassingbourn (91st Bomb Group) in mid-1944. The H2X-equipped B-17G of the 401st Bomb Squadron in the left background enjoys a maximum height at the fin of 15 feet, 6 inches—6½ feet short of its Allied cousin around the latter machine's cockpit! The Short design's sound maneuverability in flight belied its appearance on the ground.

The flight engineer was positioned on the starboard interior ahead of the forward wing-spar support frame. Ahead of his seat, positioned on the fuselage side, was the large box frame containing the engine and fuel monitoring dials, gauges, etc. Behind the seat are the starboard pair of wheels, the small one controlling cabin heat and the large example operating the starboard wing fuel jettison valve.

No. 623 Squadron's operational career was short (August 10–11 to December 4–5, 1943), in which period 150 bombing and minelaying sorties were flown, for the loss of ten aircraft. Mk. III EF156/IC: E is under inspection after being downed during a Gardening sortie off the Frisian Island chain. The crew's fate is unknown, but the intact state of the airframe suggests some or all survived the incident.

The strain is temporarily over, and an anonymous No. 90 Squadron crew can settle down to talk over the latest op to Berlin with the debriefing officer. Unknown to them is that the Stirling's career within Bomber Command will be over within two months, primarily due to the continuing inordinate loss scale borne both by bombers and personnel (of the fifty-six crews lost, those flying Stirlings suffered a far-higher fatal casualty rate than their Lancaster and Halifax contemporaries).

A No. 90 Squadron Mk. III rises gracefully off the runway at Ridgewell; in the right background can just be discerned several B-17s that belong to the 381st Bomb Group, 1st Bomb Wing. The airfield has already been handed over to the USAAF by the June 1943 stage of this picture, but a handful of the RAF bombers remained there until the early part of the month.

Mk. III HA: N is assigned to No. 218 Squadron, but the airfield it was then parked on was certainly not her home at the time, Downham Market. The clue lies in the clothing of the airman on the left, whose attire matches that of a member of the USAAF, but which base remains a mystery. The personnel are surely impressed by the sheer scale of the bomber, if nothing else. (One American officer once commented, "If this is a Short Stirling, what does a Long one look like!")

The bare tree branches and the flat East Anglian landscape provide a barren backdrop for the Mk. III assigned to No. 75 (New Zealand) Squadron, based at Mepal. The application of maximum engine power has rendered the propeller blades invisible. The two-year spell on Stirlings ended with conversion to the Lancaster in November 1944.

The portside Hercules engines on this Stirling have their innards exposed, with three individuals engaged in working on the duo. The clothing worn by the men appears civilian in origin, so the scene could be photographed at what is a production source for the Short Co. bomber.

The Stirling shared the same rear turret as the Lancaster in the form of the FN20, which was equipped with four .303 machine guns, seen here on a No. 15 Squadron bomber manned by a Sgt. Auger. The striking power of the weapons was poor both in effect and range vis-à-vis the cannon and heavy machine gun batteries mounted on Nachtjagd fighters. The central Plexiglas panel is detached to provide vitally needed visual acuity.

Mk. III EF120 arrived at No. 1660 CU, based at Swinderby in Lincolnshire, after surviving operations with No. 214 Squadron but finally succumbed to a crash landing on March 14, 1944, which fractured the fuselage around the wing trailing edge. Ground personnel are attending to the middle upper turret and vertical fin, but the aircraft's fate as fit only for salvage is inevitable.

War correspondent McDonald Hastings is snapped as he boards a Stirling. He was one of several reporters who risked their lives in bringing back to the public an impression of what it was like to fly on operations. He survived his experience, but several of his contemporaries were less fortunate and lost their lives in the process. His son Max followed on in the same profession in the postwar world.

Two German personnel stand by the port wing of an anonymous Mk. III that has become a recent MIA casualty. The heavy impact has fractured the fuselage behind the FN50 turret, and the No. 2 engine propeller and nose turret have been ripped off. The vacant Plexiglas panel in the cockpit roof indicates use as its exit point for some crew members.

The Stirling's relegation from frontline Bomber Command service in late 1943 still witnessed the aircraft's service elsewhere, such as advanced crew training. A Mk. III assigned to No. 1564 HCU is seen in the company of a Mk. V Spitfire, while a Wellington lurks in the left background. The twin-pilot layout provided a valuable platform for trainees to be accompanied by an operationally experienced contemporary.

On November 15, 1944, Mk. III LK437, operating with No. 1657 HCU, made an emergency landing that ended just short of Ridgewell airfield, what was then the base for the B-17s of the 381st Bomb Group. The extreme proximity of the crash site to the church demonstrates how fortunate the crew were to avoid impact with the structure and survive the incident intact.

No. 620 Squadron's existence within Bomber Command was brief, extending from its creation in June 1943 until withdrawal from command operations in November. The action was followed by transfer to No. 38 (Transport) Group. The five airmen posing in front of a Mk. III appear to be both aircrew and ground crew personnel, with the flying-booted example (*right*) the sole one within the former-mentioned category.

There was an inevitable international flavor regarding those aircrew assigned to the RAF's Central Flying School, as seen here. The officer in the center wears the uniform of the USAAF, while his contemporary third from right appears to wear a lighter-colored equivalent reminiscent of the army-style clothing worn by South African personnel. The distinctive outfit on the officer second from right links him to a national air force currently unknown to the author.

PO Brown's No. 15 Sqdn. being debriefed after the Berlin op on November 24, 1943, have no immediate knowledge that the presence of the Stirling in direct Bomber Command's assaults on the Third Reich are now over. From now on the Short design will be allocated to mine-laying and supplying agents and weapons to the resistance movement within occupied Europe. A third important function will be as a glider-tug and the release of supplies for the 1st and 6th Airborne Divisions of the British army.

The No. 1654 HCU aircraft has now been caught as it lifts off the Glatton runway, with the landing gear still to commence retraction. The rather clumsy appearance of the bomber in this aerial configuration is deceptive and gives little indication of its overall maneuverable qualities when in normal flight condition.

The appearance of a Stirling at any USAAF airfield must have elicited a reaction bordering on disbelief at the massive spread of its airframe vis-à-vis any American contemporary. For instance, the cockpit height was fully 22 feet above the ground—6½ feet higher than a B-17's fin. This example is a Mk. III serving with No. 1654 HCU and was snapped at Glatton (457th Bomb Group) sometime during 1944–45.

No. 149 (East India) Squadron was the fourth Bomber Command unit to convert to the Stirling, in November 1941. The quartet of Mk. IIIs is flying a close-formation pattern in this scene. However, in practice, operations would be flown in solo fashion within a nocturnal and virtually unseen bomber stream up to November 1943.

A Stirling is being readied for an op, according to the photographic evidence, with the airman in the light coat probably a senior NCO assisting in attaching the lifting frame. The blunt-ended cylinders match those of sea mines. A pair of rectangles on the bomb bay doors are one of several fitted along the length, although their function is unclear.

Mk. III LJ560/EX: B, assigned to No. 199 Squadron, operating with No. 100 Radio Counter Measures (RCM) Group, displays a marked variation in its operational record, totaling thirty sorties. Bomb symbols are displaced by glasses of foaming beer. The beer-bottle teddy bear artwork relates to the aircraft letter. A collapsed landing gear inflicted heavy damage on August 29, 1944.

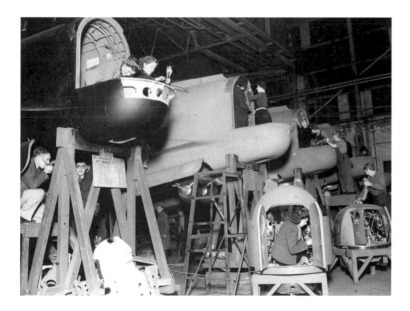

The rear end sections of four Stirling fuselages are being attended to by a group of staff who are predominately female. The aircraft variants are pure bomber in function, as proven by the FN5 nose turret (*bottom right*), which was dispensed with on the Mk. IV and V Stirlings. The role of women within British World War II production factories was unconditionally vital in the successful prosecution of the conflict.

An airman is peering from the cockpit window of Mk. III Stirling EF397, assigned to No. 90 Squadron, one of three within the photo frame. Below him on the nose section is a basic piece of female artwork, carrying a bag bearing the name "LULU." RAF artwork was generally more basic and not so risqué compared to what was displayed on USAAF aircraft. This bomber was destroyed in a crash returning from Wüppertal on May 30, 1943.

The loading-up of a Mk. III Stirling is in progress; two standard bombs, one of which is emblazoned with stickers doubtlessly indicating hostile reference to the enemy, are being complemented by a larger and arguably more high-blast weapon (*right*). The LS trolley code confirms the bomber is serving with No. 15 Squadron.

The aircrews on No. 199 Squadron, with ground crew teams behind, are lined up along with their Mk. III Stirlings at Lakenheath as an inspection by the Duke of Gloucester takes place. This Bomber Command unit transferred to North Creake, Norfolk, in May 1944 as an element of No. 100 (RCM) Group, whose function was electronic and "Window" interference with the Nachtjagd defensive screen.

A Mk. III serving with No. 199 (RCM) Squadron has performed a headstand that most likely accrued from an overshoot of the runway. The unit was based at North Creake in Norfolk, from where the crews conducted Mandrel and Window jamming sorties in support of Bomber Command.

No. 199 Squadron was assigned to No. 100 (RCM) Group during May 1944 and along with No. 171 Squadron provided cover for Main Force formations with the use of Mandrel. The aircraft flew extended racetrack patterns, with the equipment emissions forming an electronic jamming barrier thwarting all Luftwaffe attempts to pick up movements until the bombers finally emerged into the clear. A series of ventral stick aerials were fitted, but only two are seemingly visible on EX: N's rear fuselage.

A trolley accumulator for external start-up purposes, lying in the right background, is one of several pieces of equipment casually scattered around the dispersal site for Mk. III OJ: K, a No. 149 Squadron aircraft; the FN5 and FN50 turrets are shrouded against the elements, but not the FN20. The deceptively peaceful atmosphere could rapidly change should an operation be announced.

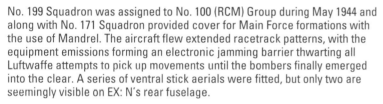

The 91st Bomb Group Base at Bassingbourn played host to numerous RAF aircraft, whose crews likely enjoyed the lavish hospitality of their USAAF counterparts. Mk. III Stirling EF403/TV: Y, from No. 1660 HCU, is parked up, with the background casting up hazy images of B-17s in what is a 1944–45 scenario. This aircraft had previously served with the Bomber Development Unit (BDU) before operating with No. 214 Squadron; note the H2S set under the rear fuselage.

The Stirling's unique though also clumsy undercarriage structure is fully revealed here. The doors are mounted at a point where the lower strut-length hinges backward. The entire mounting is retracted upward to a point where the doors line up with the engine nacelle base. The base of the wheels is exposed to the airflow following the doors' retraction.

CHAPTER 5

The overall lack within RAF ranks of custom-built transport aircraft akin to the USAAF's C-46 and C-47 equivalent designs would never be materially eased during World War II. A high-wing Avro version utilizing the wing and tail sections of the Lancaster assembled to a new fuselage structure was on hand in small numbers by 1943, but little else was available. The Short Co. had considered adapting the Stirling for this passive but vital supplementary role, which would evolve into the Mk. V. However, an interim measure involving Britain airborne divisions was put into action that was materially based on the Mk. III, apart from several adaptations.

The Russian and, even more, the German military had shown the way for these airborne troops to provide a bridgehead at weak points in an adversary's defenses that in the latter case would involve brilliant strikes by the *Fallschirmjäger* (paratroopers) in securing locations long enough for their ground-based Wehrmacht/SS colleagues to reinforce and secure such breaches. Although the burgeoning aerial might of the American transport resources could cater for the carriage of paratroopers, there was a secondary and equally important manner affecting their deployment in the form of gliders; these could carry both personnel and support equipment with which to hold their gains more readily, until relieved.

There were three glider types, one American and two British, either currently available or coming on stream, whose presence would prove vital during the long-planned invasion of western Europe under Operation Overlord. The CG4 Waco was a front-loading aerofoil that was limited both in troop and equipment-bearing terms. The Airspeed Horsa was better provisioned in both categories, but the true weight bearer was the Hamilcar, whose massive fuselage could accommodate vehicles as large as a light tank.

Where the Stirling and also the Halifax would prove valuable was in towing these gliders, rather than in the paratroop-dropping aspect; their interior layouts and especially their exit points were not up to the latter task compared to the C-46 and C-47, to whom the role was eminently suitable. By contrast, the Stirling's additional engine power was regarded as far more capable of airlifting and absorbing the aerial drag presented by all the Allied glider types (in practice, the Waco and Horsa would end up being towed by the American transports, but not the Hamilcar).

The project was initiated in April 1943, when Mk. III BK645 and LK403 were used for the tests, which proved a success, whereupon selected Mk. III airframes totaling over three figures were duly modified as follows. The nose and middle upper turrets were detached, and a curved Plexiglas frame was inserted in the former location; later airframes would incorporate a second Plexiglas panel up front between the upper and bomb aimer's Plexiglas frames. A key fitting was the towing yoke, whose flexible U-pattern structure was applied in line with the elevators. The yoke also had a central strut aligned with, and secured to, the aircraft centerline. Also fitted on the forward fuselage were twin "Rebecca" H-pattern aerials for blind-landing guidance.

The relatively open fuselage interior proved suitable for the carriage of support equipment; with this in mind, a hatch was built into the underside, just ahead of the entrance door. Also located directly behind was a tubular metal frame to be deployed when releasing the parachute-guided equipment. The rectangular frame's function was to prevent the parachute strops from fouling either the yoke or the elevators. A converse weight-saving measure was the reduction in fuel capacity from 2,254 to 1,165 gallons. The assumption that initiated this revised figure—namely, the maximum anticipated range to be flown—would prove accurate

Mk. III LK403 was chosen as a test vehicle for the glider-towing yoke, whose solid frame is fitted under the rear turret, to confirm the aircraft's function in this role. The Airspeed Horsa and even more so the General Aircraft Co. Hamilcar were sizeable aerofoils, but the No. 196 Squadron Stirling completed the experiment perfectly. LK403 later served with No. 1665 HCU but was finally written off in a landing crash after the landing gear failed.

Stirling production was particularly concentrated at the Rochester and Belfast factories, with the latter facility responsible for 1,331 airframes—over half the overall figure of 2,374. The thousandth example was a Mk. IV PK237, which has been prominently marked up with the fact directly behind the starboard wing. The aircraft survived the conflict only to be scrapped in 1946.

in practice for the three major operations destined to be launched between June 1944 and March 1945.

Further tests with two custom-adapted Mk. IVs, EF503 and EF506, confirmed the efficacy of the overall scheme, although there was another necessary adaptation, this time affecting the Hercules engines. To avoid the possibility of overheating when towing a glider at its maximum AUW, cooling fans were installed, and the "Bell"-pattern spinner covers, discarded early on in the aircraft's Mk. 1 Series 1 production sequence, were resurrected as an additional streamlining benefit, as well as being retained throughout the remaining production life of the Stirling. By December 1943, the first reportedly true Mk. IV EF317 was rolled out of the Belfast plant, although other records record LJ512 as the first example.

The conversion of Mk. IIIs to Mk. IV configuration (Plan A) was followed by production-line-arrayed Mk. IVs (Plan B). The final Short Co. proposal under Plan C was for a custom-built freight and personnel transport, the Mk. V, whose operational career would span the period on either side of World War II's conclusion. All three plans arose from mid-1943 discussions. (A maximum altitude of 19,000 feet at a 70,000-pound AUW and a range of 2,630 miles at 10,000 feet with maximum fuel capacity were also confirmed from the tests with EF503 and EF506, but their practical application would await the advent of the Mk. V.)

Airborne Operations

D-day

By June 1944, four of six squadrons within No. 38 Group were equipped with the Mk. IV; in addition, the Special Duties squadrons Nos. 138 and 161, tasked with dropping personnel and supplies to the Resistance movement, were similarly equipped, while two further Mediterranean-based units (Nos. 148 and 624) had converted to the Short Co. variant. All glider-towing flights had progressed in order, and as June 5 drew to a close, the initial phase of Overlord was being launched, with paratroopers jumping from twin-engine Albemarles to reinforce their colleagues flying in Stirling-towed Horsa gliders, all heading for key points on the eastern fringe of the invasion zone. In the case of the latter, two gliders landed close to a lifting bridge over the Orne Canal, with others covering the adjacent Orne River crossing. Their lightly armed numbers were facing a potential onrush of armor that, had these Panzers broken through the dangerously thin screen, would have raised the nightmare scenario of a second Dunkirk, rather than the initial success of Overlord that thankfully evolved on the morning of the sixth. A mix of skill and fortune saw the

positions held until substantial reinforcements arrived. Closer to the eastern coastal fringe, other paratroopers neutralized several heavy-gun batteries whose fire would have posed a serious threat to Allied vessels aligned off the landing beaches.

Market Garden

The success of D-day was tragically not repeated three months onward, when a plan to cross the Rhine by seizing bridges between Eindhoven up to the key example at Arnhem, fording the mighty water barrier, was dispatched on September 17. The US 82nd and 101st Divisions were assigned the bridges along the route, while Britain's 1st Airborne Division took on Arnhem under what was named Operation Market Garden. The British 2nd Army would drive up the corridor, with the intention of advancing into Germany and encircling the Ruhr industrial complex to nullify the area as a major producer of arms, prior to sweeping relentlessly on into the German interior. Thus would the fervent hope for a conclusion to the conflict be achieved before the end of 1944.

All went well initially at other than Nijmegen, and even there the bridge was secured in time. The Arnhem units were dropped 7 miles distant due to the mistaken belief that unsuitable marshy ground surrounded the bridge. However, two Panzer regiment remnants from the Normandy campaign were refitting close by and, realizing what was happening, rushed through enough tanks and infantry to effectively bar any progress farther than the bridge's northern approach. The bright hopes for the operation had just received its first rebuff. This fact, along with stubborn German resistance along the corridor, ensured that the intention to reach Arnhem within two days was thrown completely out of kilter. Even had the Dutch town been reached, the delay ensured the overall timescale achieved was to prove too late; by then the British paratroopers' gallant bid at the bridge was over, as the enemy forced them ever back and into a steadily shrinking perimeter.

Attempts over the six days up to the twenty-fourth to fly in supplies to the besieged men were carried out by C-46s, C-47s, and Mk. IV Stirlings, in what was effectively an aerial death trap as a solid flak battery cordon poured a weight of fire upon the aircraft, forced to fly a steady and low course over the battle area. In the case of the Stirling crews, ten were MIA on the nineteenth, with another eleven the next day, and a seventh of the force, sent on the twenty-first, never returned. By the twenty-fourth a further thirty-six crews were absent from their airfields, representing over half of the 112 Stirlings on hand within the six No. 38 Group squadrons prior to the seventeenth.

The flat territory allowed some pilots to carry off crash landings, but the overall human casualty rate was still high and was matched by their contemporaries in the C-46 and C-47 participating units. Adding to the tragedy was the ground radio sets within the perimeter failing to transit far enough to be picked up by the aircraft; coupled with the ever-shrinking defensive perimeter, the result was that much of the equipment never reached the defenders. The paratroopers known as "the Red Devils" from their maroon berets had fought determinedly but were simply overwhelmed; by the twenty-fifth, two thousand survivors had crossed the Rhine to reach Allied lines, and two thousand were dead, with the remaining six thousand facing imprisonment or, in a few fortunate cases, finding shelter with the local population.

The breaching of Germany's formidable marine barrier of the Rhine was finally commenced on March 24, 1945. Once again, the Allied parachute regiments spearheaded the way by dropping on key positions. No. 38 Group's contribution involved 143 Mk. IVs towing Horsa and Hamilcar gliders carrying men from the 6th Parachute Airborne Division. Their specific objective was Hammenkiln, and the zone was occupied within hours. However, unlike during the two previous major operations, the ground defenses took a heavy toll of the gliders, and the parallel result was a high level of human casualties.

Although the Stirling fully matched up to the requirements for towing heavy gliders such as the Horsa and Hamilcar, there was an inherent risk of engine overheating with the standard Hercules engine layout. Cooling fans, the blades of which can be seen on the port outer engine of an anonymous Mk. IV, were fitted into the forward cowlings as a perceived antidote.

The paradrop hatch on the Mk. IV has been opened and the tubular metal frame that acts as a parachute strop guard is lowered, the latter acting to prevent the strops, two of which are twisting out in the airstream, from fouling the elevators. The glider-towing yoke directly behind the tailwheel doors is clearly depicted.

Two extended lines of Mk. IVs are arrayed along one of the runways of a No. 38 Group airfield. The full application of D-day stripes confirms that within hours, the crews—among whom will be the airman casually leaning against an aircraft's starboard main wheel—will be initiating the aerial aspect of Operation Overlord. The unit is believed to be No. 299 Squadron.

Prelude to the tragedy. These members of the 1st Parachute Brigade appear in high spirits, to judge by the reaction of the tall figure toward the left. Behind them is a line of Mk. IV Stirlings and a solitary Horsa glider ready to transport them to Arnhem in Holland. The date is September 17, 1944. Within nine days, one in every five of the 10,000-strong force will be dead, with three of every four remaining survivors becoming POWs.

The Horsa glider has been loaded up with troops and equipment and is now attached by towing cables to its Mk. IV tug. A handful of army personnel wave to the glider, bearing cutback D-day stripes on the ventral fuselage and wing areas. It is commencing the takeoff run, as indicated by the taut nature of the cables. Operation Market Garden with all its tragic portent is under way.

The Mk. IV was perfectly capable of towing any Allied glider up to the massive Hamilcar, and the picture picks out an Airspeed Horsa with its four-engine tug. The apparent absence of D-day markings on the Stirling's wings and a reduction on the glider's fuselage suggest that the picture was shot during Operation Market Garden, launched on September 17, 1944, an action whose glowing promise was primarily swamped within the ruins of Arnhem.

The increasingly urgent need to resupply the British 1st Airborne Division within the steadily shrinking enclave at Arnhem ensured that the RAF transports would face the full fury of German flak, since they flew a low and steady course. The result was a severe loss factor among the participating aircraft. A crash-landed No. 196 Squadron Mk. IV has had the port wing severed and sustained heavy damage to the rear turret, among other damage, with the fate of the crew unknown in this instance.

A total of ten squadrons in all, with six assigned to No. 38 Group, would operate the Mk. IV. In No. 295 Squadron's case, the switch to this Short Co. variant occurred in July 1944 and ended with unit disbandment the following June. The 8E codes were applied to "B" Flight aircraft. A total absence of D-day stripes suggests that the photo was shot during the final months of World War II.

An anonymous Mk. IV Stirling features a group of individuals either embarking or disembarking from its interior. The presence of the Plexiglas panel in the central nose was a refinement added only as the production sequence evolved. Propeller spinner covers and cooling fans within the cowling fronts were other specific items applied to this variant.

The bomb-bearing character applied to the fuselage of a Mk. IV Stirling is backed by the aircraft's pilot. The aircraft has flown twenty ops, as denoted by the dagger symbols, which likely relate to supply arms drops for various resistance groups within occupied Europe, who challenged their Nazi oppressors in any way possible while awaiting Allied liberation.

This Mk. IV serving with No. 195 Squadron is seen taxiing on the inboard engines, an action usually made after landing off a flight. The large-scale P7 code letters in use here were a general exception within No. 38 Group.

Mk. IV Stirlings from No. 620 Squadron are flying a finger-four formation, a pattern more reminiscent of Fighter Command tactical procedure. The reduction of D-day stripes indicates a late summer date. The reduced size of the squadron code letters compared to the aircraft letter was a unit specialty; their grouping together was an enforced change thanks to the stripes application around the rear fuselage.

The ruined buildings (*far right*) and revolver worn by the signal-lamp-bearing RAF sergeant are clear indications that the picture was shot on the Continent during the final stage of World War II. The absence of D-day stripes on the No. 299 Squadron Mk. IV add to that impression. Wire bundles are most likely Summerfield tracking, ready to be deployed for temporary runway layouts. Interestingly, the aircraft still bears type A1 markings despite these having been comprehensively superseded by type C1 equivalents from mid-1942 onward!

The enveloping mist of the winter of 1944–45 is accurately caught in this picture of a combined aircrew / ground crew group posed by their assigned Mk. IV, which bears minimal D-day stripes on the fuselage. The photo angle conceals the squadron codes, but the nose displays an interesting variation in operations symbols. Among them are two windmills, probably relating to Operation Market Garden, the daggers cover SOE drops over France, and mountain artwork relates to Norwegian-directed operations.

The same Mk. IV is liberally festooned with a gathering of aircrew and ground crew personnel, some perched perilously on the engine cowlings and fuselage nose. Additional artwork depicts a parachute-borne beer glass and appropriate slogan underneath. The glider on the middle-row end is for Operation Varsity, the Rhine crossing on March 24, 1945, while daggers with the Danish flag at bottom confirm operations over that country.

This picture of a party of young boys was reportedly taken at Prague in 1945. The two Mk. IV Stirlings are likely both with No. 570 Squadron; V8 was one definite unit code combination, as seen on the near-side aircraft, from which another youthful party is gathered around the entrance door, and the other was E7, with the visible letter on the far-side machine lending credence to its assignment to this same squadron.

A trio of Mk. IVs serving with the Central Navigation School at Summerside in Canada start up their engines sometime in June 1944. The presence of H2S equipment is a necessary fitting, at odds with the variant's normal transport role but relevant to their function here. The aircraft in the foreground is reportedly LK589, which returned to the UK and served with Nos. 295 and 570 Squadrons out of Rivenhall.

"Just Jane" was a newspaper cartoon character ever prone to losing her clothing in parlous circumstances. Here she adorns the fuselage of a Mk. IV from No. 295 Squadron. Included with the daggers for SOE operations are two gliders, confirming towing operations. The aircrew and ground crew groups are probably depicted at the end of World War II, given the tree foliage in the far background.

A line of Mk. IVs with a B Flight aircraft from No. 299 Squadron on the right forms the backdrop to a group of British army personnel. It is unclear whether they are former POWs or not, but the presence of kit bags would suggest the latter. The aircraft were used to transport POWs back home or, conversely, to fly regular troops out to the Continent.

The waters of Lake Röjdåfors in western Sweden have become the final resting place for Mk. IV LJ899 from No. 190 Squadron; the fuselage has fractured directly behind the cockpit, the FN5 turret appears to have taken the brunt of the impact, and the no. 3 propeller is missing. The aircraft was ferrying troops to Norway on May 10, 1945, when it went out of control. The aircraft was one of two lost this day, with all on the second killed when it came down near Oslo.

What is either a late-war or postwar scenario has a Mk. IV Stirling that is seen in the company of at least two turbine-powered Meteor fighters, among other aircraft in the background. The absence of machine guns in the rear turret likely denotes that the Short design had been withdrawn from further frontline service and could even be heading for the scrapyard.

Other Operations

The activities by SOE in providing supplies to the Resistance groups as well as parachuting in agents, which had initially involved the Mk. III prior to D-day, was also taken on by the Mk. IV. A practical aspect of the flights involved the bomb aimer assisting the pilot up to the point of crossing in over the enemy coast; he then moved down into his compartment to commence his map-reading role. Once the flights were on approach to the briefed drop site, the prearranged signals between the aircraft and those on the ground were indulged; any deviation would result in the pilot aborting the operation. The bomb bay and rear ventral hatch were involved, depending on the equipment container proportions. The slim, round containers could more easily be stowed in the bomb bay, whereas basket-sized or similar items would be loaded within the fuselage and dropped through the hatch.

Arguably the easiest-paced, not to say pleasant, duty was conducted immediately following Germany's surrender. This involved the repatriation of British POWs. Most of the flights were centered on Brussels, Belgium, where the men had been assembled. Later during 1945, similar repatriation flights were conducted on a broader geographic scale, this time around involving personnel eligible for demobilization. A steady disbanding of squadrons was being initiated around this period, and by March 1946 the retirement of the Mk. IV from RAF service was similarly reaching its conclusion, leaving only the Mk. V as the Short Co.'s heavy-transport participant alongside the Avro York within RAF ranks.

A Scottish regiment bagpiper and a soldier from another regiment lead a party of paratroopers from the 1st Airborne Brigade away from one of the Mk. IV Stirlings that have brought them to Norway shortly after the German surrender in May 1945. The act of liberation for the inhabitants, who had borne Nazi occupation for over five years, was titled "Doomsday."

No. 570 Squadron had participated in Operation Overlord, operating on Armstrong-Whitworth Albemarles, but converted to Mk. IV Stirlings during July. A pair of Stirlings are seen taxiing around, presumably for takeoff. The squadron's first major operation was Market Garden, which cost it dearly, with nine aircraft shot down along with twenty-two crew fatalities. Following World War II's conclusion, disbandment occurred in January 1946.

CHAPTER 6
Mk. V

Mk. V PJ943 was one of forty-five airframes produced between September 1944 and March 1945. The aircraft's parallel position to the photographer shows off the revised camouflage scheme of dark green and medium gray above and either light gray or azure blue below. The conclusion of hostilities witnessed a switch to bare metal or white paint on later production airframes, however.

The final Stirling variant was officially predicated upon its function as a freight/passenger aircraft whose operation would extend beyond the conflict into which it was born. Specification C18/43 was duly responded to by the company whose design staff utilized Mk. III LJ530. The nose compartment was reshaped to feature a sloping upper surface, with the entire section hinged at the top to permit loading; a Plexiglas nose panel was also fitted. The section was raised and lowered using a beam block-and-tackle frame aligned along the upper nose. The middle upper and rear turrets were detached; in the case of the latter, an extended rectangular fairing took its place. The twin vertical reinforcing ribs applied to the outer edges became standard on airframes only after the prototype and the first two production airframes (PJ878/879).

Loading of large cargo items was made via the starboard rear fuselage, into which was built a door measuring 9 feet, 6-inch by 5 feet, 1 inch, stretching back from just behind the bomb bay. The door was hinged at its base and formed a loading ramp when opened; two metal rods supported the door when in operation. The central fuselage window layout was changed to eight (port) and seven (starboard), with a respective close grouping of four and five located around the wing roots, where passenger seats were positioned. Alternate window dispositions showing eight on the port side of some aircraft, for example, have been captured on film.

The interior was cleared of all equipment relating to active operations, and seating was installed in twin rows from the rear wing spar / support frame back as far as the loading hatch. The floor surface beyond the bomb bay that dropped down on the bomber variant was covered over and raised up, to accommodate the seating as well as the loading of cargo, vehicles, etc. An interesting adaptation was the replacement of the standard tailwheels with the antishimmy Marstrand units applied to the Lancaster and Mosquito. Their presence ensured that any tendency to swing on takeoff or landing would be canceled out. However, the increased size of the wheels merited the fitting of bulges into the Mk. V door frames.

Power was provided by the Hercules XVI, with a 1,635 hp rating. With empty and all-up-weight calculations of 43,500 and 70,000 pounds, respectively, maximum speed was established at 280 mph and range at 3,000 miles, along with a service ceiling of 18,000 feet. Passenger capacity would be up to forty, a figure limited in practice to fourteen, given the standard seating installed. A further six seats could be fitted when transporting paratroopers and their equipment, while twelve stretchered patients could be added to the normal capacity of fourteen seated patients when the aircraft were indulging in medical evacuation duties.

Order numbers were set at 160, with the initial pair of production airframes being dispatched in May 1944 to No. 23 Maintenance Unit (MU) at Aldergrove, Northern Ireland. Camouflage was still a mandatory factor, but with a noticeable alteration vis-à-vis the Mk. V's bomber contemporary. In place of the subdued colors in regular Bomber Command use, there appeared a lighter combination. Dark green and medium gray was applied to the upper wings and the top and sides of the fuselage, with the undersides azure blue. Shortly following World War II's conclusion, the camouflage gave way first to an overall silver and then to a bare-metal equivalent. The weight and drag reduction accruing from this act was to increase the cruising speed to 190 mph.

A color view of a Mk. V Stirling provides a better impression of the revised late-war camouflage scheme of dark green, medium gray, and azure blue. It has replaced the extremely subdued shades hitherto applied to RAF multiengine aircraft, with the separation line applied to the upper fuselage and wing surfaces.

The urgent need for a national airline in Britain witnessed company tests with PJ985 that foresaw a thirty-passenger capacity variant and soundproofing added to the fuselage. The prospect of attracting a contract from the World War II–established British Overseas Airways Corporation (BOAC) was unfortunately to remain stillborn. This was due to the Handley-Page Co.'s Halton, an adaptation of the Halifax with a detachable ventral freight pannier under the bomb bay, catching the eye of the BOAC authorities to the extent of their granting the contract in that entity's direction. A further nail in the Mk. V's civil aviation coffin arose from Avro. The advent of the C Mk. II Lancastrian, developed out of the Lancaster, provided a passenger-carrying facility with a superior range (4,150 miles), maximum speed (310 mph), and altitude (23,000 feet) for the RAF. Indeed, it was destined to outlive the Halton for several years. Avro furthermore was designing a true custom-built civilian airliner in the form of the Tudor.

A close-up view of the same Mk. V picks out the Plexiglas nose cone and the starboard "Rebecca" H-pattern blind-landing aerial. The aircraft is sharing the anonymous airfield with a C-47, as well as a B-17 stripped of its top turret and serving in a secondary, nonoperational role.

Mk. V Stirling PJ987 was assigned to No. 242 Squadron and is photographed sometime in mid-1945. The lighter camouflage pattern along with the underwing type D roundels are indications that the global conflict is at or even beyond the point of conclusion; in fact, the latter situation is more likely, since the aircraft came off the assembly lines as the seventeenth airframe after production commenced during April.

A Mk. V Stirling presents a good image as it makes its final landing to an anonymous airfield approach sometime in January 1946. The ZO main fuselage codes confirm its assignment to No. 196 Squadron. The overall bare-metal finish was typical of late-production airframes, although some were reportedly sprayed in white.

Mk. V Transport

Wingspan	99 ft., 1 in.
Length	90 ft., 6¾ in.
Height	22 ft., 9 in.
Empty weight	43,500 lbs.
Maximum weight	70,000 lbs.
Powerplant	Four 1,650 hp Bristol Hercules Mk. XVI air-cooled radial engines
Armament	None

Performance	
Maximum speed	280 mph at 6,000 ft.
Cruising speed	233 mph at 11,000 ft.
Climb rate	800 ft. per minute
Service ceiling	18,000 ft.
Range	3,000 miles
Crew	5

PK125 was assigned to No. 51 Squadron and is seen at an airfield in India; for whatever remote reason, the Mk. V is being pushed along with a single individual behind the rear, adding to his colleagues' efforts up front. Note the exhaust pipes, which are repositioned lower down the cowling frame, and the outline of the cargo hatch.

The twin ramps are in position and a jeep is in the process of being driven into the Mk. V's interior. The sizable dimensions of the cargo door still leave the driver with a tricky task of maneuvering his charge within the restricted fuselage interior while simultaneously avoiding any damaging contact with the vulnerable airframe.

No. 46 Squadron was stationed at St. Thomas Mount, an airfield in India, when this takeoff incident involving Mk. V PK173 occurred. The collapse of the landing gear has resulted in damage to the Gouge flap structure, and the vehicle mounting a heavy crane will be involved in raising the aircraft up. The crew were fortunate the aircraft did not veer left and impact with the hut structure in the background, a collision that could have had fatal consequences.

In May 1947, twelve Mk. V Stirlings were sold to a Belgian company, Trans-Air. Six were converted into passenger-carrying aircraft carrying thirty-six passengers, and six as freighters. OO-XAS was one of the last in the group, and her fully civilian status is clearly defined, with no evidence of her original bomber or even military status evident.

A companion Mk. V to OO-XAS is OO-XAK, which is clearly in pristine condition. The location is more tropical in nature, to judge by the light clothing worn by the individuals gathered around the aircraft. All twelve aircraft were withdrawn from service within twelve months. A Mosquito lurks in the left background.

The fuselage of a Mk. V has had its fuselage interior adapted to carry personnel. There are twin rows of padded seats ahead of the cargo hatch (*right*), with at least two more seats visible (level with and behind the hatch). The V-pattern frame up front forms the base of the rear wing-spar support frame. The nonpressurized interior would have proved rather noisy on extended flights, especially those to the Middle and Far East zones.